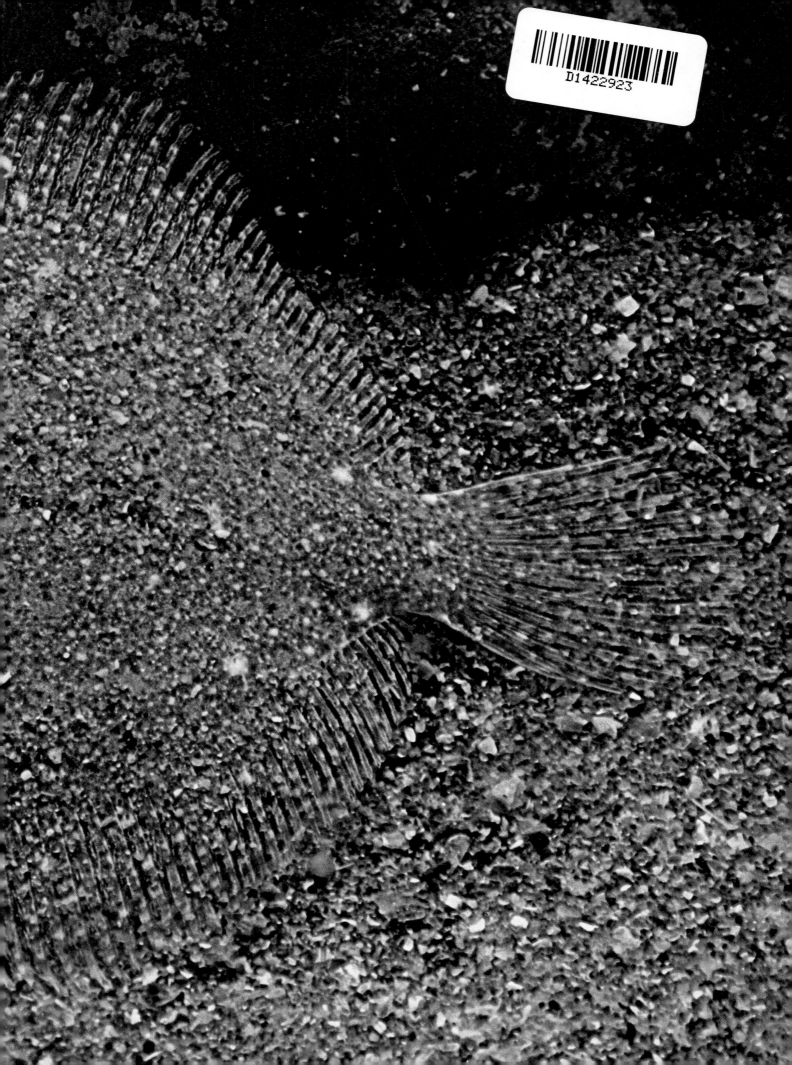

D1422923

The World You Never See
Underwater Life

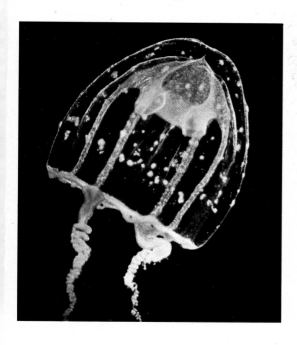

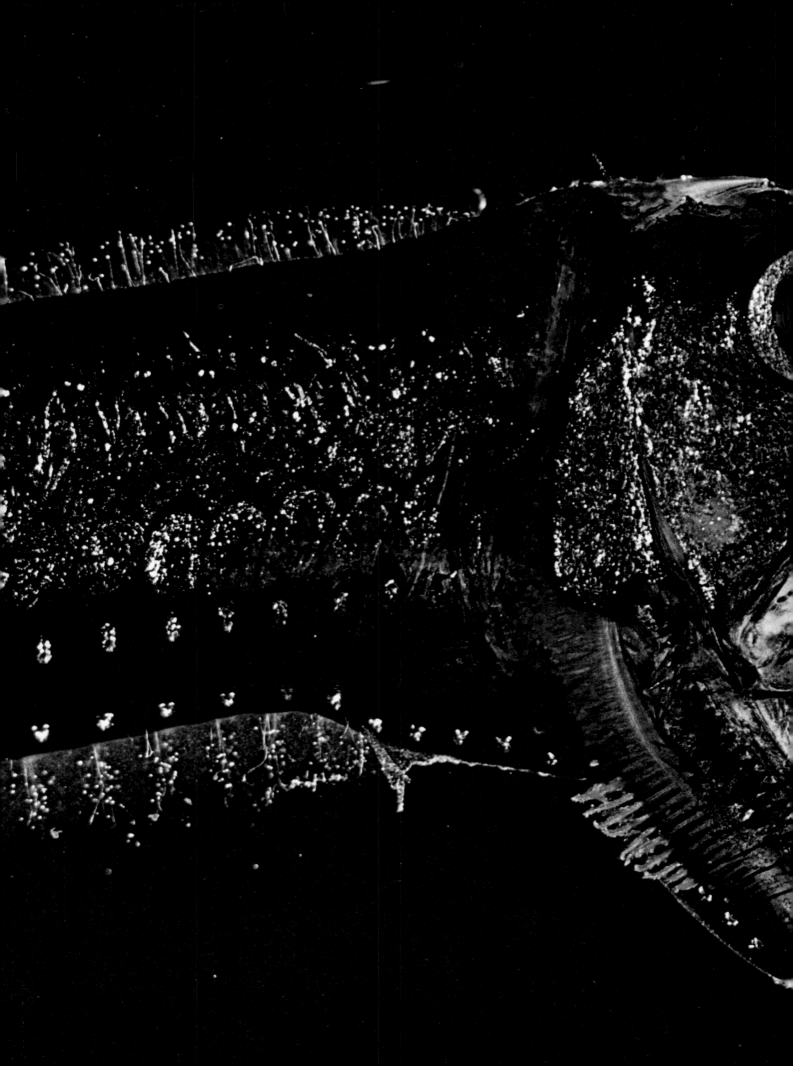

The World You Never See
Underwater Life

Written and photographed by
Peter Parks, BA, FRPS
of Oxford Scientific Films

Hamlyn
London · New York · Sydney · Toronto

Contents

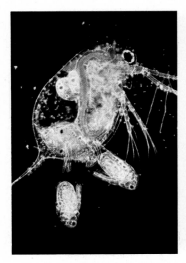

Published by The Hamlyn Publishing Group Limited
London · New York · Sydney · Toronto
Astronaut House, Feltham, Middlesex, England
Designed and produced for the Hamlyn Publishing Group by
Intercontinental Book Productions
Copyright © 1976 Intercontinental Book Productions
Colour Reproduction by Starf Photolito s.r.l., Rome, Italy
Printed in Italy
ISBN 0 600 39358 5

Foreword

Only very rarely do I write a foreword to a book, because as a rule I feel one is unnecessary; here, however, I could not resist the invitation for the selfish reason that it gives me so much pleasure to add a few words to this splendid volume from Oxford Scientific Films.

My pleasure is multiple: for one thing the subject has always held a fascination for me, and much of it links with my own field of research; then I have the greatest admiration for the work of OSF in general; more particularly, the main author of the book is my pupil Peter Parks who has written all but the chapter on the seashore life, which is, however, by another of my pupils, John Cooke; and a further reason, indeed the most important one, is the quality of the photographs — the great majority by Peter Parks — which are remarkable not only for their combination of scientific interest and artistic beauty, but also for the inventive ingenuity by which they were obtained. Although not shown here, Peter's coloured drawings of animal life are as good as his photographs, and it is surely this gift that gives such an artistic quality to the composition of the latter; as for his inventiveness, just look at some of the pictures of his equipment, all designed with much trial, and I've no doubt sometimes with tribulation, to overcome the difficulties in hand.

The text is not intended to be a comprehensive biological statement. Whilst it introduces the general reader to so many different facets of underwater life and describes some of the extraordinary new facts discovered, it does something else: it conveys the adventure and excitement of hunting out these secrets of nature and — often after frustration and much patience — bringing them back as 'living' pictures. The reader cannot fail to be caught up in the enthusiasm — yes, the joy — of these explorations and recordings. Chapter 2 opens with these words: 'Capturing rarely seen biological phenomena on film for everyone to witness is one of the greatest joys of wildlife photography'.

The foundation of Oxford Scientific Films was triggered off by Gerald Thompson's classic and award-winning film on the private and hidden life of the wood-wasp and its parasites which made history in the field of scientific cine-photography. All along it has been largely concerned with revealing 'the world you never see' — maybe inside a log of wood, as in the wood-wasp film, or the world that can only be seen through a microscope, or aspects of animal life which cannot be seen except by the use of the slow-motion film as in OSF's brilliant studies of the hovering flight of humming birds or again, as in this book, the underwater life. If the real value of the work of OSF lies in the presentation of moving pictures of active living creatures, what merit, it may be asked, has such a book as this — one which consists of still, isolated moments snatched from their stream of action? It must be confessed that they are not the same; the book, however, is the next best thing and this is where the text comes in, for it is based on first-hand observations made as the films were shot. It describes the movements you cannot see, such as the remarkable calliper and pincer-like action of *Amoeba* in capturing an active prey; or how a water-flea, in a fraction of a second, is sucked into the lethal bladder of the underwater plant *Utricularia* which feeds like a carnivorous animal, or again, how the water-flea itself captures its food and gives birth to living young.

I am sure the book will bring great credit to OSF and make the general public still more hungry for its films of the world you never see. I wish it every success.

Sir Alister Hardy, FRS, Emeritus Professor of Zoology, University of Oxford

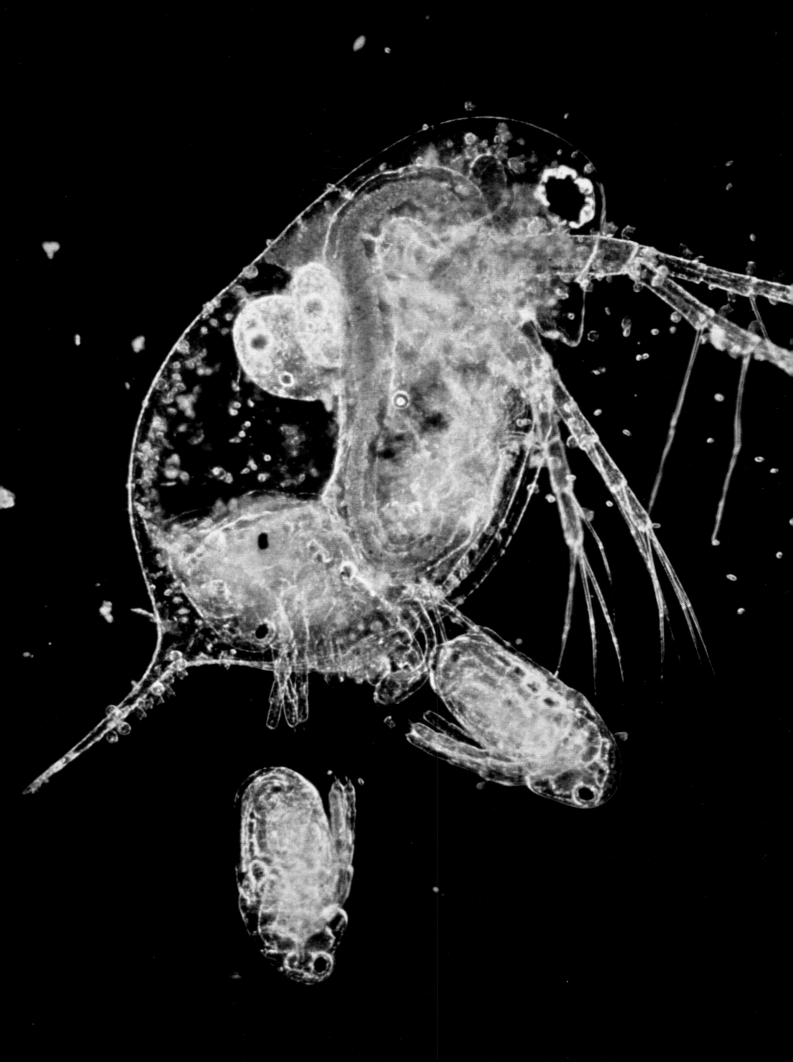

Chapter 1

Life in a Drop of Water

A dewdrop seen in a spider's web is a remarkably pure form of natural fresh water. Yet if a splash drop from a rising waterfowl were caught in the same web it might contain hundreds or even thousands of incredibly small life forms. These life forms and those of some much larger organisms, such as water-fleas, which depend upon them for their daily food, are the subject of this account. To the creatures capable of living within it, the drop is like some vast geodetic dome. Most of the animals and plants described here are microscopic, and their world is hard both to imagine and to research, yet the little that *is* known suggests that ecological principles apply here every bit as much as they do in our own environment.

The most notable character in the drop – the water-flea – is in fact like a juggernaut compared with the other occupants, which you will not be able to see with the unaided eye. But it is with these smaller inhabitants that we are initially concerned.

Water butts and ditches often contain water that looks like pea soup. Among the simplest of the single-celled organisms, or protists, that could be responsible for the colouration is a spirally-swimming, light-loving, solar-energy-harnessing, starch-storing species called *Euglena*. Simple though this minute animal-plant is, it displays a remarkable level of development within its flexible outer coat or pellicle. Like all good plants (or most of them at least) *Euglena* contains a chloroplast which enables its owner to absorb solar energy, and then to utilize this energy source to construct its own complex tissues from relatively simple building materials like water, carbon dioxide, nitrates, nitrites and phosphates. Lodged neatly, and very distinctly, within the chloroplast, are two ring-doughnut-shaped objects. These are believed to be starch-storage organelles. The way in which they operate is far from understood – possibly starch is stored by plants, as is fat by Arctic and Antarctic mammals, as a survival kit when more normal energy supplies give out, or become impossible to claim.

The means by which *Euglena* species propel themselves through the water is rather remarkable; they skull themselves along with a whiplash, called a flagellum. Have you ever tried manoeuvring under water with a bull whip? I doubt it – but it

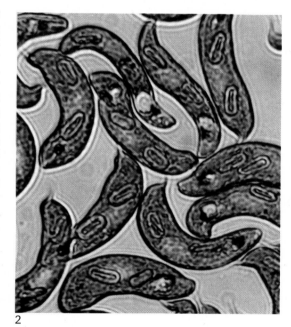

2

1. *Daphnia* giving birth.

2. The green stagnant look of waterbutts and garden ponds is often caused by the presence of millions of single-celled animals with plant-like qualities, called *Euglena*.

would be rather difficult! However, a vast range of single-celled animals get along very well with just such a piece of equipment. Some direct the flagellum out in front of their cell body, and so pull themselves along. Others direct the flagellum down the side of the cell and then flail it behind them – thereby propelling themselves in a spiral path.

Eyes and evolution

Invariably linked with the base of the flagellum is an orange spot, said to be light-sensitive and hence termed an 'eye'. It is believed that the 'eye' is in fact made up of two discrete organelles. One of these, the orange-coloured spot, is thought to cast a shadow upon the eye proper, which is set off slightly to one side. As the creature spirals its way through life, the shadow of the spot is repeatedly cast upon the eye, which thus receives a type of passive scan of the light intensity of its surroundings. A radar scanner sees a bright spot moving over a dark background: a flagellate 'sees' a darker spot moving over a bright background. How this information is relayed to the controlling 'centre' of the cell, and then interpreted into actions by the flagellum, may well be a mystery for many years to come. It is fair to say, however,

1

3. When the green colour of pond water is not the result of *Euglena* being present, it is very likely that a single-celled motile alga called *Chlamydomonas* is responsible.

4. As if eight chlamydomonine cells had joined forces and become closely linked in the form of a minute rotating ball, algal colonies of *Pandorina* swarm at the surface of a pond.

5. *Eudorina* takes *Pandorina*'s colonial habits still further. In this species as many as thirty-two or sixty-four chlamydomonine cells reside within a gelatinous sphere, leaving only paired cilia projecting to the exterior.

6. Seldom if ever before shown in true size relationship to one another, the volvocine algae, *Chlamydomonas*, *Pandorina*, *Eudorina*, *Pleodorina* and *Volvox* sit side by side in an enlarged, multiple exposure 16-mm frame.

3

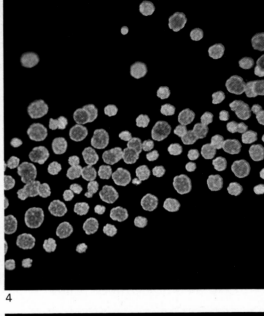

4

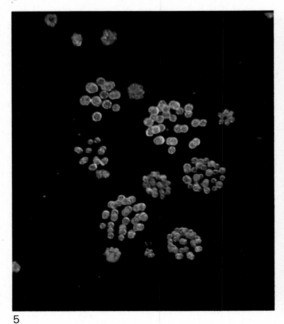

5

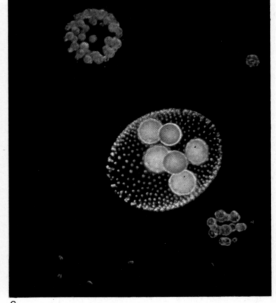

6

that one would be hard pressed to design a better control-system in a car, let alone in something as small as a blood corpuscle.

Many of the basic characteristics discussed with regard to *Euglena* and its compatriots are pertinent also to the volvocines, like *Volvox* itself, and its smaller cousins, *Pleodorina*, *Eudorina*, *Pandorina* and *Chlamydomonas*. All can turn a water butt's contents pea-green and all tend to be high summer blooms, but there is one overriding fact above all that makes these algal species interesting. They represent a series of elaborations which may suggest a way in which single-celled organisms became multicellular in the dim, evolutionary past. It is convenient, but probably quite wrong in terms of evolution, to imagine the single-celled *Chlamydomonas* associating with others like itself, and so forming a colony of eight cells as in *Pandorina*. By each cell doubling-up, an organism like *Eudorina* could arise, and by trebling or quadrupling-up, a pleodorinid algal colony could evolve. In the case of *Volvox* the doubling-up process has occurred

time and time again and colonies containing several thousand cells have arisen. In these larger species the colony takes the form of a hollow fluid-filled sphere. The component cells of the stroma, or outer surface, are embedded in a gelatinous envelope. Through openings in the envelope each parent-colony cell subtends two flagella, which by beating in synchrony with their neighbours, result in the indescribably beautiful progression best described as 'rolling through space'.

Daughters and desmids
All mature, reproducing *Volvox* individuals give rise to what are termed daughter colonies. Amazingly, while these dense, green daughters mature within parents, granddaughters may start to develop within daughters. It seems rather hard to be born pregnant! Before being released, or born live, to the outside world of pond and puddle, daughter colonies roll free of the inner wall of the parental sphere and gently orbit around, like

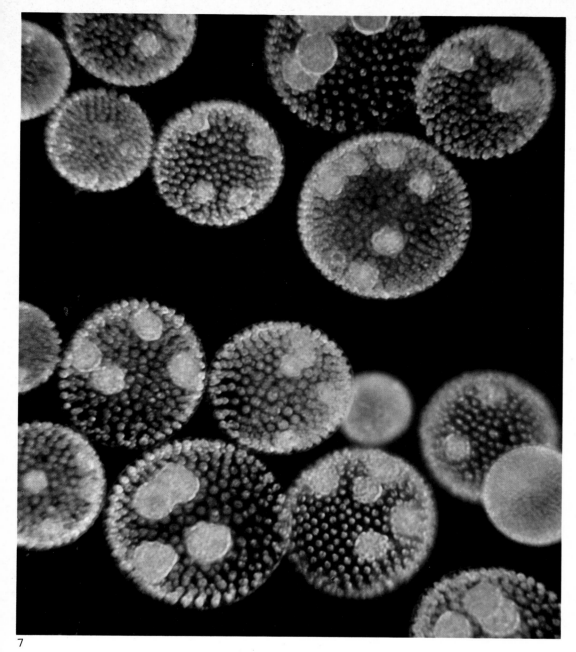

7

7. Like Chinese chessmen with their bases containing balls within balls, parent *Volvox* colonies contain daughter colonies which, in turn, may contain their own second-generation daughter colonies.

epicyclic gears within a gearbox. Within hours of this mobility becoming apparent, the wall of the parent colony ruptures, and one by one, out drift maybe as many as ten daughters, to start a new orbit in the microcosm of the infinitely small. Meanwhile the spent parent colony, with side gaping, drifts erratically down to the pond bottom, where it becomes just one tiny particle of the decaying leaf litter, compost and sludge that floors all stagnant waters.

Amidst decaying plant materials little green cigar-shaped structures are sometimes found. Some are straight; others are bent, so they look rather like bananas. They are all called desmids, but further than that, they are somewhat enigmatic. We know they are plants, but we do not understand why some of them bloom at a time when most plants wither and die. Nor do we know why they are invariably found on and around decaying plant tissue. We know they are toughly coated, like their relatives the diatoms, but we do not know why their outer layers have minuscule

pores. We know that they move slowly but surely and yet we are not sure how this gradual progression is achieved.

Movement amongst microbes is a subject beset with mysteries and in no animal is it more strangely displayed than in *Amoeba*. The contents of an *Amoeba*, viewed through the transparent 'skin' or ectoplasm, appears granular and lumpy. Most of the grains are crystals believed to be products of metabolism, but specific to the species of *Amoeba* in question. For the most part the lumps are food vacuoles: that is, pockets of engulfed animal and plant material in various stages of intracellular digestion. One lump is itself granular and is the nucleus. This is the reproductive control centre of the cell. Frequently, a clear spherical area appears and disappears repeatedly, at a point within the granular cytoplasm. This clear sphere is the *Amoeba*'s 'kidney', or water control-system. It is a law of nature that liquids flow from where the concentration is greater to where it is less, when the two liquids in question are separated by a semi-

8. Live birth is not confined only to vertebrate animals. *Volvox* develops daughter colonies within the plant colony and ten or more may be born in rapid succession by 'breech birth'.

9. Desmids, belonging to the genus *Closterium*, cluster in and around decaying plant material like green Churchillian cigars. Population explosions of *Closterium* often occur in late autumn and winter.

10. *Spirogyra* is easily detected by its slimy texture when handled. It is a common filamentous alga which, in mid-summer, may clog stagnant freshwater ponds.

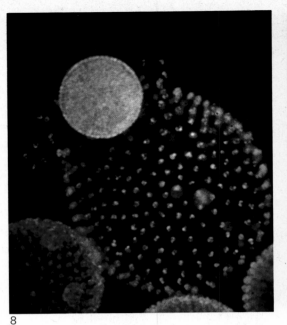

8

9

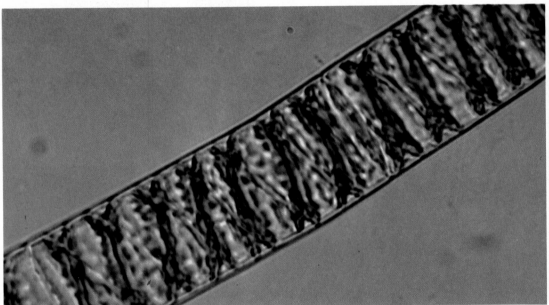

10

permeable membrane. Most natural membranes are semi-permeable. Skin, for example, is no exception. Long-distance swimmers don't grease their skins to keep warm: they do it to prevent excessive uptake of water. Exactly the same problem faces any animal living in water, be it salt or fresh, although freshwater animals in general have a more severe problem than those living in the sea. The system found in *Amoebae* to prevent uptake of water is the contractile vacuole, and it operates by discharging excess osmotic water every twenty minutes or so.

Amoeboid anatomy

Mention has already been made of other vacuoles such as the food vacuole, found in *Amoeba*. Indeed *Amoeba* can boast some strange facts about its food vacuoles and its eating habits in general. Since the food-capture process relies to a large extent upon one aspect of its locomotion, we must first consider how *Amoeba* gets around. As might be expected, being a gelatinous creature of

indefinite shape, its mode of progression is rather different from most of its fellow creatures. If you agitate the water in which amoebae are living, some will float free from the substrate underneath them. Within a minute or so, they will have extended arm-like processes in all planes of space. This serves to emphasize two very important points about amoebae. One is that having no defined limbs or locomotory processes, their entire surface can operate as a limb, or limbs. The second is that they are essentially three-dimensional animals. You might ask how they could be anything but three-dimensional, but ask most biologists to draw *Amoeba*, and the chances are they will give you a two-dimensional outline with not the slightest reference to its third dimension, or 'depth'. Having spent many years filming amoebae of different species, I am well aware that many textbook pictures and verbal accounts are blatantly at fault, in both general description and biological detail. As such textbooks abound, I would like to concentrate here upon those aspects

11

11. Like something out of a science-fiction story, amoebae and nematode worms flow through and between fungal hyphae surrounding decaying barley grains. In this, its native environment, *Amoeba* is both hard to find and impossible to study.

12. A recently developed illumination system picks out the nucleus of *Amoeba* as a dark blue area which is usually close by the dark contractile vacuole.

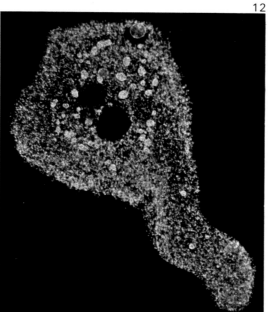

12

of this unique life form which are never seen, or, if they are, in my opinion, are often incorrectly described or interpreted.

It is true to say that the exact way in which *Amoeba* moves is still not known. Many learned papers have been written on the subject, yet still no satisfactory explanation exists.

In filming feeding reactions in *Amoeba proteus* at OSF, we have found one or two unusual facts. Firstly, *Amoeba proteus* appears to 'measure', with a two-dimensional calliper-configuration, a potential victim of its own size or greater. Secondly, it is capable of engulfing a swarm of as many as thirty very active, free-swimming ciliates within one food vacuole. Thirdly, it seems to react only to flagellar or ciliary beat, and yet, on one occasion in five years of observation one specimen was seen to engulf completely a piece of dead filamentous alga three times its own average length. The alga continued to deform the *Amoeba* during the several hours it was under observation. Food vacuoles normally do deform the *Amoeba* a little.

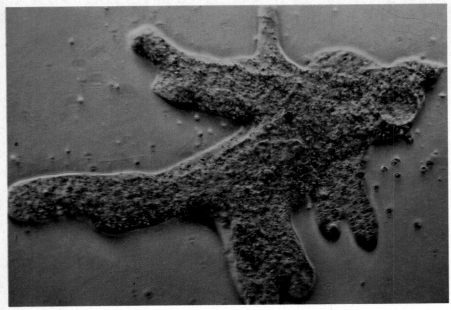

13

13. A rather extreme form of interference illumination is the only photographic system which emphasizes the three-dimensional nature of *Amoeba*. The contractile vacuole looks like a crater.

14. The cytoplasm of *Amoeba*, when viewed with dark-field illumination, becomes a galaxy of coloured food vacuoles and white crystalline storage products. Together they cluster around the dominant nucleus and contractile vacuole.

15. Seldom if ever before seen to engulf dead plant material, *Amoeba* must now be listed as an occasional scavenger. A strand of filamentous alga grossly distorts its devourer.

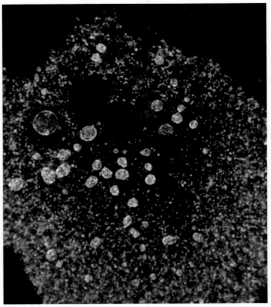

14

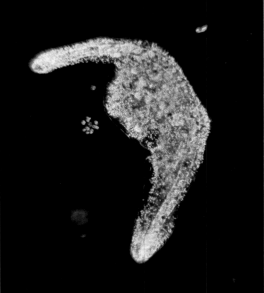

15

In the case noted above, in which a single *Amoeba* captured a complete swarm of ciliates, these were carried in a large blister-like vacuole, held high above the creeping soul of the beast. One was vividly reminded of an angler with a keep-net, full of his catch.

One further intriguing observation we made while filming *Amoeba*, was that when the animal appeared to measure a potential victim, the climax to the calliper-formation was marked by a sudden muscle-like jerk which opened the jaws of the calliper quite appreciably. This is particularly remarkable as *Amoeba* is said not to possess muscle-like fibrils or myonemes.

Amoeboid gastronomy
While considering the feeding habits of *Amoeba* it is worth mentioning the story which, for me, so clearly demonstrated that ciliary stimulus was necessary to trigger off a complete feeding reaction. While watching a mixed culture of amoebae and rotifers, or wheel animalcules, as they are called, I noticed that several amoebae contained rotifers within their food vacuoles. Most of the rotifers were still very much alive and were writhing around, reminiscent of children under bedclothes! I was just thinking how strange it was to see multicellular animals devoured by unicellular ones, when I noticed a looping rotifer approach an *Amoeba*. It continually bumped, prodded, and jostled the *Amoeba*, but all the while its ciliary corona was withdrawn and in the inverted position. Finally it settled with its cement gland on, or very close to, the *Amoeba* and started its characteristic unfolding of the corona of cilia. It then waved gently to and fro, filtering into its jaw-like mastax a current of food-containing water. Suddenly the corona cilia brushed the side of the *Amoeba*. From the point of contact the *Amoeba* immediately sent out pseudopodia, which rapidly took up the food-engulfing pattern, as they streamed towards the rotifer. The rotifer in fact looped away just in time, but for me there was little doubt that it was the cilia that stimulated the *Amoeba*. For the next few hours I searched for similar encounters. Time and time again I saw the same thing happen, and occasionally, capture ensued. Some months later I saw the same thing with eudorinid algae and with ciliates.

One of our commonest ciliates, though one not taken by *Amoeba*, is *Paramecium*, the slipper animalcule. It is no exaggeration to say that *Paramecium* resembles a slipper. It actually looks like one of those soft leather slippers traditionally sought by office-worn husbands. The hole where the foot would enter is, in life, the gullet or mouth of the beast. The 'toe' is the slightly streamlined hind end of the cell and the 'heel' and 'sole' are represented by the anterior end of *Paramecium*, which is slightly twisted.

Paramecium's blue nucleus
The twist in the cell body gives rise to the very common protist feature of spiral progression. Propelled by thousands of synchronized beating cilia, or hair-like cell extensions, *Paramecium* prescribes a course through the microcosm of late summer and autumn like a faulty ballistic missile!

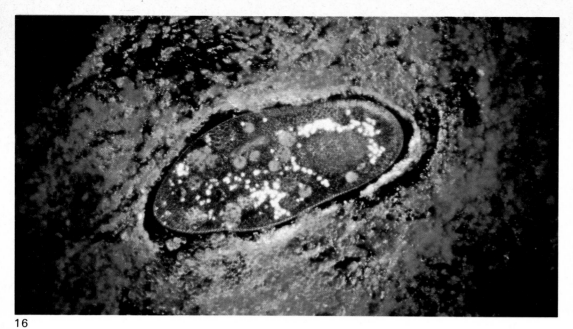

16

16. When placed in a culture of yeast stained with a vital acid/alkali indicator reagent, *Paramecium* readily feeds upon the yeast cells and so demonstrates its digestive-tract activity.

17. The incorrect use of a thirty-year-old lens has revealed otherwise invisible features of ciliates, like *Paramecium*, in detail which is both beautiful and instructive. The nucleus appears sky-blue.

18. Yeast cells turn from orange to magenta when alkali displaces acid digestion. One of two dark contractile vacuoles fills and empties near the light blue mega- and dark blue micro-nucleus.

Unlike the missile though, *Paramecium* can either gently swing into a new trajectory, or even totally reverse its flight path. All this it does by re-synchrony of those beating cilia.

Although outwardly so different from *Amoeba*, *Paramecium*, and indeed the other ciliates discussed in this chapter, consist of just a single cell with a nucleus, a granular cytoplasm, an ability to engulf victims, a crystalline cytoplasmic component and, a feature more markedly apparent than in *Amoeba*, a prodigious ability to reproduce asexually. The nucleus can in fact be further defined as consisting of a larger, day-to-day control-centre or meganucleus, and a smaller reproduction control-centre known as the micro-nucleus, which is tucked into one side of the meganucleus. In OSF we have been lucky recently to hit upon – by luck more than by design – a rather unusual lighting system that displays the nucleus of all ciliates as a Cambridge-blue object. In fact it is only the meganucleus that is rendered this shade of blue – the micro-nucleus, or *sex* coordinator, is rendered Oxford-blue! This system of illumination is still not fully understood. Though shown to the Royal Microscopical Society no one seemed to be able to provide a definite explanation. It was however agreed by two physicists at the meeting that the likely solution was a suggestion made by an old student colleague – namely that the blue colour was a shattering Tyndale-blue effect.

There is a chemical staining procedure which can be used to good effect with *Paramecium*, enabling us to monitor not nuclear activity, but digestive activity. *Paramecium* has a predilection for yeast cells. If yeast is permitted to stand in a solution of powdered Congo red dye for about ten minutes, before a healthy swarm of slipper animalcules is introduced into it; then, viewed under a microscope it will not be long before the ciliates start to feed avidly upon the red-stained yeast. Large food vacuoles, containing scores of yeast cells each, appear within the cytoplasm of the paramecia. Gradually, these yeast cells become purple and then prussian blue. This gradual change of colour indicates progression from acid

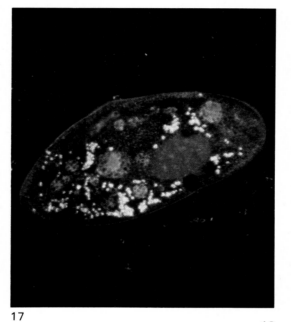

17

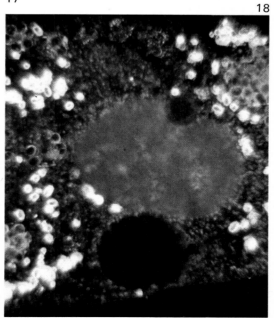

18

19

19 To feed, *Stentor* attaches itself to a substrate with an adhesive 'gland' and extends its ciliary corona and vortex-like gullet into the protist and bacteria-laden waters.

20. *Stentor coeruleus* and *S. polymorpha* look like a mass of miniature ear-trumpets as they suddenly appear amongst the rotting organic debris of autumn. Only two or three weeks later, just as suddenly, they disappear again.

20

digestion to alkali digestion, within the single cell.

The paramecium's gullet is lined by a tough ectoplasmic pellicle, leading to a patch of naked cytoplasm at its inner end. A row of special fused cilia waft yeast cells, and the like, into the gullet and down towards the cytoplasm. Once in this little vestibule the cytoplasm engulfs the food cells rather in the same way as *Amoeba* does.

Shelling *Stentor*

Of all the protists so far discussed none can be considered as spectacular as *Stentor*. Most characteristic of the autumnal dying-off period, *Stentor* will be detected by the nose as well as the eye! Nothing can be quite so pungent or nauseous as the smell arising from a November pond; a pond which in summer abounded with greenery and quivered with the wealth of animal life. The smell is produced by bacteria. It is the protists and rotifers that filter these diminutive life forms from their surroundings that comprise the staple diet of *Stentor*.

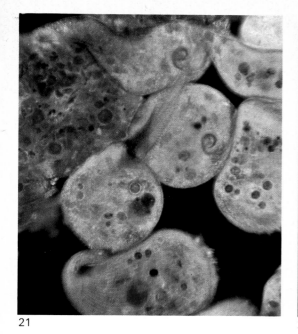

21

22

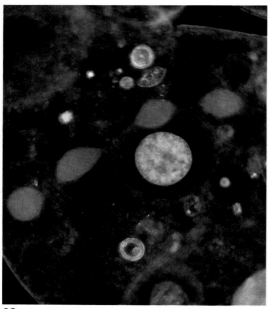

23

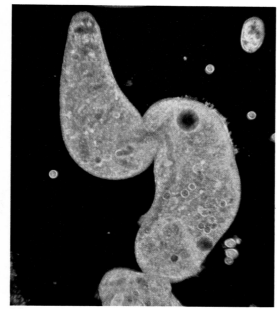

24

On the OSF premises, in mid-November 1974, we suddenly noticed that our freshwater keep-tank had an exploding population of *Stentor* forming. The water was milky and putrid, and the tank itself black and scummy, but to the *Stentor* this was heaven! A single scrape along the edge of the tank with a bulb pipette, which was then injected into a small beaker of water, produced a living soup. Under the microscope the sight was incredible! The entire field of view was a seething, writhing mass of two species of *Stentor*; the big purply-blue *Stentor coeruleus*, the largest freshwater ciliate in the northern hemisphere, and the green alga-containing *Stentor polymorpha*. Amongst the *Stentor* swarm, there were rotifers, *Coleps* ciliates, *Paramecium*, and a host of green flagellate unicellular algae. Upon all of these, *Stentor* were avidly feeding; some could be seen to contain several writhing rotifers – themselves multicellular. Others had algal victims, while several had made their meal of one or two *Coleps*. *Stentor* will even feed on young water-fleas.

Ear-trumpets and dustbins

Only a few minutes were needed to pick out several dividing *Stentors* from this mêlée. Unlike *Paramecium*, which divides end to end, *Stentor* seems to divide *en echelon*. In fact it is end to end, but the point of attachment seems to be off-centre. A late-stage, dividing *Stentor* looks exactly like two ear-trumpets, the earpiece of one inserted shallowly inside the trumpet of the other. To add to its attractive colouring and indescribably supple manoeuvrings, *Stentor* has a corona of large, rhythmically-beating cilia which lead into a vortex-like gullet. The perfect synchrony of the beating cilia leads to the deceptive impression that the trumpet-end of the animal rotates. This, coupled with the extraordinary, detailed sculpturing all over the surface of *Stentor*, gives one the impression of looking at a well-oiled machine, not an animal at all.

Stentor of all species differ from most other ciliates in that they are amazingly versatile. They cement themselves to a surface and set up feed-

21. When seeking new feeding sites, *Stentor* round off into globular creatures, almost as if trying to occupy as small a space as possible. They then insinuate their holdfasts into suitable anchorages.

22. As *Stentor* shifts its feeding activity from one site to another, it detaches its basal holdfast and swims free. It is then propelled by its entire ciliature as well as its feeding corona.

23. Unique dark-field-illumination techniques show the cell contents of *Stentor* to consist of multicellular and protist animal and plant food vacuoles, as well as the spectacular 'string-of-sausages' meganucleus.

24. Asexual reproduction in *Stentor* is by simple binary fission. Owing to its asymmetrical design, however, the 'Siamese-twin' stage of division looks more complicated than in other ciliates.

25. Sexual reproduction in *Stentor* is by conjugation; the process in which 'male' and 'female' individuals come together and in which the nuclear content of one enters the other, to form a zygote nucleus.

26. Like bread mould on an old crust, vorticellid ciliates add a bloom to the decaying leaves of subaquatic vegetation when other flowers have withered and died.

27. Contractile, spiral stems enable *Vorticella* to withdraw from danger as well as to flush and refresh the surrounding food-laden aquatic environment. Bacteria and dinoflagellates constitute the main diet.

28. Chemosensitive papillae protrude from a lip which forms a water-flea's mouth, while an oscillating multi-lensed eye scans the microcosm ahead. A cellular lattice structure is both skeleton and overcoat.

29. *Simenocephalus* is a heavy-bodied species of water-flea which favours grubbing amongst bottom debris and detritus for its unicellular food. All species of water-flea are adapted to slightly different ecological niches.

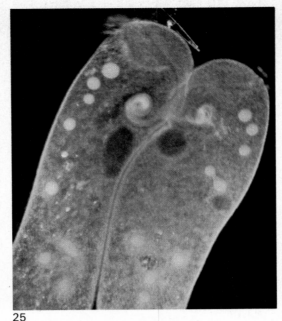

25

26

27

ing currents that draw in all sorts of creatures from distances twice their own length away. They can swim in circles like a flaccid balloon. They can swim with decided directness and accuracy, and they can squirm through microcosmic jungles like snakes. The typical feeding position is as an extremely elongated trumpet or more accurately, a coaching horn, cemented at its base and slowly swaying, with corona rhythmically beating the waft victims into that whirlpool feeding current. On disturbance however, *Stentor* contracts into a globular mass from which it only very cautiously re-opens. This contractile behaviour is reminiscent of other similar animals found in this microcosm. The unusual features of *Stentor* are further enhanced when viewed under the OSF dark-field illumination system. The blue-nucleus effect shows beautifully. The meganucleus is to be clearly seen as a string of narrowly-linked blue sausages. When 'male' and 'female' *Stentor* unite in the nuptial bliss of conjugation, the individual sausages are seen to dissociate and group into units of two and three. The complement belonging to the 'male' partner then slowly passes to the female, whereupon the sexual act is complete.

Because of its extreme activity in autumn, *Stentor* is indeed one of the best examples of the 'dustbin brigade'. Without this band of refuse-exploiters, one dreads to think what would have accumulated on land and in water during the course of the world's history.

Vorticellids and water-fleas
The last animal to be discussed here is *Vorticella*. Like *Stentor* it is a partly sessile, filter-feeding consumer of late summer and autumn decaying matter. It has many close relatives which are more characteristic of high summer. While filming in the wetlands of Wisconsin several years ago, OSF came across a beautiful bright green vorticellid, clustered around the tiny rootlet of a piece of duckweed. The whole colony – for that is the great feature of the vorticellids – continually contracted and expanded as if ducking from a low-level fighter attack.

The colony's activity closely resembles an almost simultaneously sprouting and withering tree or shrub. On one memorable occasion, when inspecting our holding tanks for ciliates, we came upon what looked like perfectly rounded masses associated with each sessile colony. Each mass was 3 to 5 cm across and appeared to be limited by a thin membrane. This later proved to be an optical illusion produced by extremely precise 'formation swimming' being carried out by the peripheral individuals within the mass. The whole mass turned out to be a swarming cloud of free-swimming, stalkless 'male' vorticellids. Later they were seen to disperse and amass about sessile colonies. Though we did not actually witness it, we presumed these 'males' were searching for 'female' partners amongst the sessile individuals. We could only imagine that conjugation – the nearest thing to sexual reproduction – would ensue.

One of the most frequently encountered small animals in fresh water is the water-flea. There are dozens of species and dozens of close cousins,

28

but all are enormous in comparison to those creatures we have so far discussed. In size, a water-flea to *Amoeba* is like an elephant to a dog. Most water-fleas and their relatives, like copepods and seed shrimps or ostracods, are in one way or another filter-feeders, and it is the organisms described earlier in this chapter that are the materials usually filtered. Water-fleas and copepods usually filter amongst debris and detritus, and so filter-off bottom-living species. It is commonly known that dried water-fleas, or *Daphnia*, are fed to goldfish. It is probably less well known that the rusty red patches on ponds in summer are invariably caused by enormous population explosions of *Daphnia*. However, even fewer people will know that water-fleas produce youngsters by live birth, are able to regulate numbers of offspring to environmental conditions, lay resistant winter eggs by casting their skins, and take in food through their back passages.

Water-fleas are now known to follow a life-cycle not unlike that of greenfly or aphids. Much

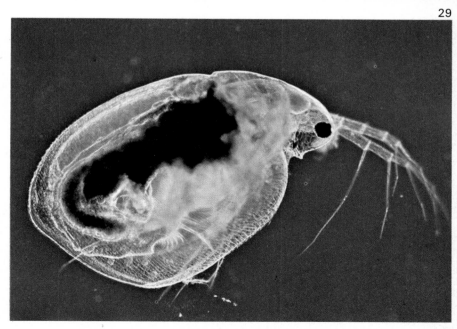

29

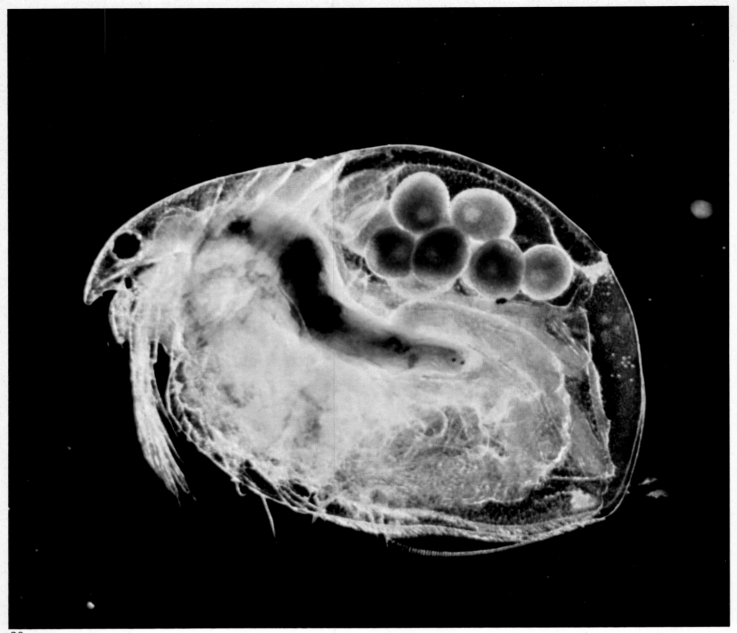

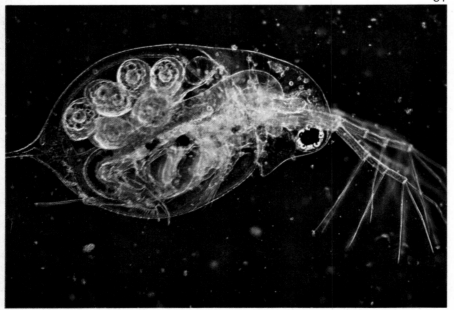

of the year, from spring to late summer, the *Daphnia* population consists mainly of females. Each female is able to reproduce parthenogenetically and few male water-fleas are seen. Female water-fleas develop up to ten or twelve eggs within special, dorsal brood pouches. These eggs are said to bear a relationship to the conditions prevailing at the time of 'conception'. If conditions are good, many eggs are produced; if poor conditions exist, few eggs seem to appear. One could even imagine a situation where a jar of water-fleas might replace the legendary seaweed to forecast weather! Be that as it may, the development of eggs, within the brood pouch, is a sophisticated process, as is proved when the eggs develop into live, swimming and kicking embryos.

Live birth

At an appointed time, these juveniles are released into the outside world. The procedure for release is an intriguing series of events which can be adequately depicted only on cine film, but which is fairly explicitly shown in the plates on page 21. The brood pouch is normally sealed by a spur on the tail end of the abdomen. At the time of birth, the end of the abdomen is flexed up and down and, at each down strike the inrush of water seems to stimulate the young water-fleas to swim and kick frantically. This rather random activity soon leads to one of the youngsters swimming towards the open end of the pouch. From this position the final expulsion is completed when, on the next body flexure, the spur on the top edge of the abdomen literally hooks out the embryo and jettisons it to the exterior. The whole procedure is particularly entertaining if an embryo gets its shoulders stuck in the entrance of the pouch, since in that position it flails its antennae, madly 'treading water', but getting nowhere fast!

One of the intriguing details we learnt from filming all this is that pregnant female water-fleas are able to enhance the survival of their offspring if they themselves should become caught by a predator. Rather as a fighter-pilot ejects himself from his damaged aircraft, a female water-flea can eject her offspring prematurely if, say, *Hydra* stings her, or a damselfly makes a grab at her.

This sort of birth process continues throughout the summer until, for a reason not yet completely understood, a generation of diminutive males and large females is produced. The males may be few in number and small in stature, but their life is not all bad, for it is their responsibility to make up for all the lack of sex through the previous ten months! It is upon their activity that the vitality and adaptability of the race depends. It is rare enough to find male *Daphnia*; it is rarer still to witness mating, and we think that OSF's filming of the mating process is perhaps unique. Part of the mating sequence we were privileged to see and film has since been incorporated into a feature documentary film for general release.

Winter eggs

As weather conditions and dietary conditions become more severe, towards the end of the summer and the beginning of autumn, the female water-fleas start to show signs of meeting the tough months ahead. Broods dwindle in size and a patchy darkening of the brood area occurs. The dark areas soon turn to sepia brown or jet black and it is possible to discern that four patches are present. They occur in pairs on either side of the creature's brood pouch, like two pannier-packs slung one behind the other. These dark patches are ephippia, or 'winter eggs', and the way in which they are shed into the outside world is extremely strange. Although the ephippia appear in the region of the brood pouch, they are not actually in it; not even lining its walls. Instead they are formed in very close association with the exoskeletal skin of the water-flea. We have our skeletons within our bodies, in the form of bones. Water-fleas have their skeletal or supporting material outside their body in the form of a tough, chitinous coat. Unlike our skeletal bones, the coat of a water-flea does not grow with its occupant, except when very soft. A water-flea's skin is soft only immediately after it has been renewed or ecdysed. Hence growth in *Daphnia* is in

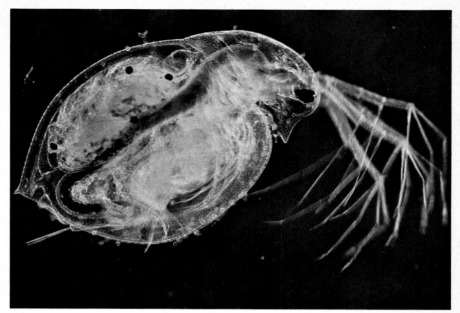

32

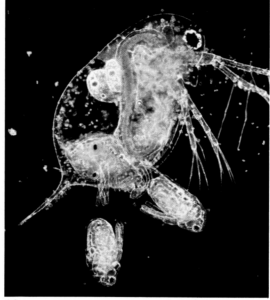

33

a series of spurts every time a skin is cast, and this may occur every week or so if conditions are favourable. Knowledge of this helps to explain why water-fleas shed their ephippia in a strange way. They simply cast their skins, and the associated 'pannier-pack' ephippia are cast too. In so doing the little black-bodied creature once again becomes pale. One water-flea can repeat this process several times. Thus in the face of adversity water-fleas actually manage to proliferate, albeit only potentially. The success of this potential population increase depends upon the survival ability of the ephippial eggs, and a winter, however clement, exposes all pond life to rigours way beyond our imagination. Nonetheless, hazardous though a water-flea's life may be, their success is irrefutable, and so the reproductive cycle described is clearly less precarious than we might otherwise assume.

(Note that the photographic sequence illustrating this process of reproduction in water-fleas continues overleaf.)

30. Egg-brooding *Chydorus* water-fleas seem to attain highest population numbers in early and mid-summer, when they scuttle rapidly over the surface of vegetation, filtering in protist algae and diatoms.

31. Some of the more pelagic water-fleas belong to the genus *Daphnia*. Throughout most of the year females parthenogenetically incubate eggs, which develop to be born as live young.

32. Water-flea eggs develop within a dorsal brood chamber. The number of eggs produced at any one time is said to be proportional to the clemency of the parent's environment at that time.

33. With frequent contortions of the hind end of the parent's gut, the exit to the brood chamber is opened and the young water-fleas escape.

34

35　36

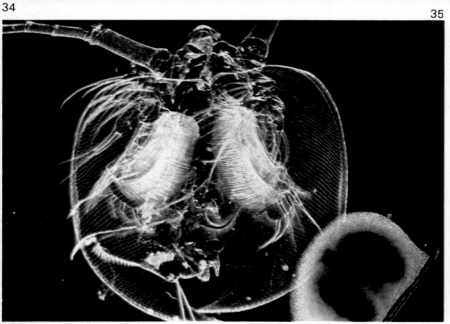

22

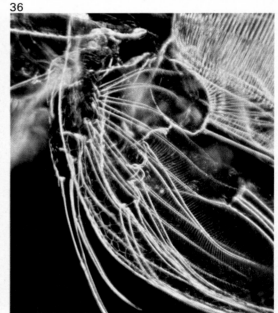

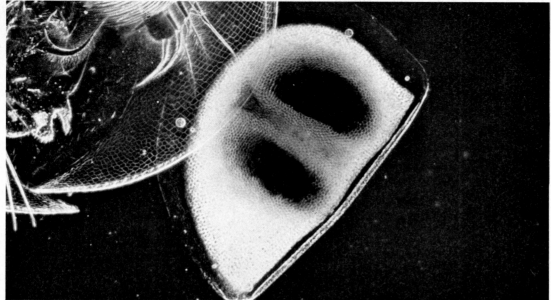

34. *Daphnia* has an amazing ability to overcome unfavourable climatic conditions. If the parent is forced to succumb, it leaves behind it black, pannier-like, resistant ephippial or winter eggs.

35. To lay the ephippial egg sac the parent water-flea sheds its entire skin, which covers every intricate surface of its body, including part of the lining to its gut.

36. The cast skin of *Daphnia* is a garment of incredible detail and beauty. It reveals the intricate design of the delicate filtering limbs, gill plates and mouthparts.

37. *Daphnia*'s egg pannier develops in close association with the skin. When it is shed the ephippial eggs either drift free and sink, or if shed in the surface film, remain there.

38. *Cyclops* is a crustacean relative of water-fleas. Females retain and carry eggs in sacs, from which, in due course, the naupliar larvae emerge and swim free.

37

38

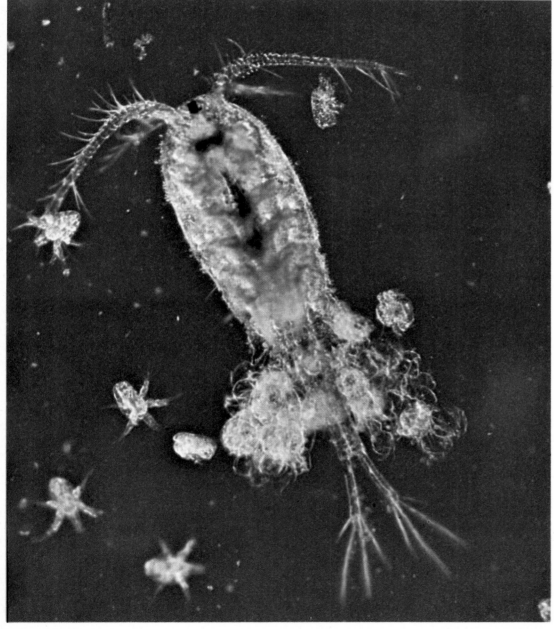

Chapter 2

The Unseen Life of Pond and River

Capturing rarely seen biological phenomena on film for everyone to witness is one of the greatest joys of wildlife photography. There are two particularly exciting and rewarding aspects of this. One comes from filming a new or exceedingly rare species and some or all of its behavioural quirks. The second is the experience of discovering and recording some hitherto unknown adaptations or behaviour pattern of the better known or more familiar species. It is the second category which seems so often to apply to our filming studies of the wildlife of pond, lake and river.

A comparatively simple example from this second category occurred recently, when we were engaged in filming the spawning behaviour of common perch. Although we knew that most fish species sleep at night, it was a revelation to see perch asleep standing vertically on their tails. The frontispiece to this chapter shows this sight as we witnessed it one morning in our tank room.

Similarly we found that perch have quite a sophisticated schooling behaviour. It appears to be in connection with this that the enormous dorsal fin and its colour-reversing posterior black spot are used. Although we do not understand the full significance, the spot and state of fin erection seem to suggest signalling. Even catching perch provided us with some strange facts, as we witnessed for the first time the extreme efficiency of the somewhat puzzling perch trap. This is best described as being similar to a wire netting lobster pot. No bait is placed within; no integral moving part entices or traps the fish, and yet this empty, funnel-mouthed trap caught as many as sixty perch in a 24-hour period. Why the perch – a fish-eating predator – should enter and remain within such a device we just do not know.

A fish with certain habits in common with the perch is the awesome pike. *Esox lucius* is a species of pike common to Britain, Europe and the United States of America. Five other species, of which the muskellunge is the largest, are also found in the USA. The rod-caught record of the muskellunge stands at approximately 31.7 kg, while the angling record for British pike is approximately 21.6 kg. Undoubtedly larger specimens await capture! No other fish can be confused in appearance with the pike. The elongated body has the dorsal fin set far back, near the extremely muscular tail. The capacious jaws are formidably

armed with sharp recurved teeth. The roof of the mouth also carries teeth, but these are hinged to bend back as prey is swallowed. The general impression given is one of speed and menacing predacity. The pike lurks among weed, its mottled colouring merging so well that it is perfectly camouflaged. From there it makes a sudden rush to seize an unsuspecting victim which swims past.

The pike is a solitary fish, except during the breeding season when two or three males assemble round a female. My colleague, Gerald Thompson, has seen as many as five males courting a large female which could have eaten any one of them, for the males seldom exceed 2.7 kg and the female is usually much larger. In fact the pike's main enemy is other pike, since they readily eat their own kind – a gruesome activity we have filmed in OSF more than once. They are often found bearing deep wounds which could have been inflicted only by another pike.

Fisherman's tale

Gerald well remembers his first capture of a pike over 9 kg – the target weight of the pike angler! He and friend were fishing a river on the last day of the season, using roach as live bait. Several hours went by with no success, until at last his friend caught a small pike of 1.3 kg which had a gaping wound, obviously freshly inflicted, at the base of the tail. The fish was returned to the river in the hope that the wound would heal, as would probably be the case. About forty metres downstream, Gerald threw his bait in under a willow tree and took his eyes off the float while he lit a cigarette. On looking up he saw that the float had disappeared; about twenty seconds later it came to the surface on the other side of the river. He struck immediately and was into the fish; at once he knew by the resistance that it was either a large fish or a submerged tree! After several seconds of immobility, the pike (for so it was) began to cruise, in quite a leisurely fashion, up and down the river.

So far Gerald had not seen the fish, but after about five minutes it thrust its head out of the water and, with open mouth, shook itself violently. The sight of such a big fish was awesome and more by instinct than conscious action, Gerald dropped the rod tip to relax the line, which otherwise would have been likely to snap. He was now in no doubt that this was his largest pike ever and this was con-

39. It is now well established that fish sleep, although their eyes remain open. Many assume sleeping colours and sleeping postures and perch may sleep standing on their tails.

40. The greatest potential enemy to a small pike is a large pike, which may in turn fall victim to a still larger pike. Frequently the victim has itself just taken a fish.

41. Unquestionably one of our filming highlights was the night the brown trout first spawned in the specially constructed river tank. We had never before seen this classic, mouth-agape posture.

40

41

firmed when he netted it after another five minutes, to find it weighed 10.6 kg. Unfortunately Gerald had to kill his capture since the hook had been taken down into the stomach and a lingering death would follow if he cut the trace. Out of curiosity Gerald examined the stomach contents. There were four items, of which the largest was a pike 45 cm long, perfect, except for some digestive action on the head. Presumably the fish had only recently been swallowed since the stomach juices of the pike act extremely quickly. Secondly there was his roach bait, and it seemed surprising the pike had taken this when its stomach already contained a very large meal. The third and fourth items were even more unexpected; they were two linen bags, each 20 × 12.5 cm, with the words 'Wiltshire Sausages' printed on both sides, on one bag in blue ink, on the other in red.

In the western world, angling is a favourite recreation of a very large number of people. In recent years much attention has been paid to increasing facilities for fishermen; worked-out gravel pits, for example, have been stocked with trout, carp or pike. Pressure has been brought to bear to reduce pollution in rivers which formerly held high stocks of fish. Much of this pollution, however, comes about through other leisure activities. The increase in sailing, and particularly the cult of the cabin cruiser, has increased pollution in some waters to a degree which fish cannot tolerate.

Tank and trout

Fish management, as with any form of animal husbandry, must depend on a sound knowledge of the ecological requirements and this means that all elements of the aquatic environment must be taken into account. All too often, man tries to favour the animal in which he is particularly interested by upsetting the natural balance between plants, herbivores and predators; the result is inevitable failure. It is essential to work *with* nature, not *against* it, and this realization has given tremendous impetus to the study of ecology during the last two decades.

42

42. The thrill of the trout spawning was eclipsed some weeks later by the breathtaking sight of a wild dipper flying beneath the water to retrieve the fertile trout eggs.

43. John Paling's concept and Ian Moar's engineering attained fruition in November 1968: the OSF river tank has enabled cameras to record some miraculous wild-life events.

Our experience of filming brown trout spawning gives some idea of the attention to detail which is necessary to ensure success. Although it is possible to take pictures in a trout stream, the lack of variation in camera angle, the natural cloudiness of the water (even though it appears at first glance to be clean), and the variation in light, mitigate the possibility of producing high-quality pictures. We therefore decided to try to use a studio tank with artificial lighting and to film through the glass sides. To this end, we built a tank 2.7 metres long through which filtered water could be pumped at a controlled speed. Feeding the fish was no problem since trout readily take special pellets. But in order to simulate conditions conducive to the trout we had to know such things as the speed of water flow, the temperature of the water, the nature of the river bed and the depth of the substratum in rivers they favour. We had to decide, too, whether there was a need for local currents within the tank.

It was also essential to predetermine the place where spawning would occur, so that the cameras could have an uninterrupted view. We soon found that it was necessary to pump about 4,550 litres of water through the tank each minute, to achieve the rate of flow of a trout stream. Temperature was somewhat more difficult. Trout spawn in late winter when the water is cold – about 4°C. Our tank being in a heated room, we had to include a cooling unit in the system, otherwise the fish would rapidly lose breeding condition. The bottom of the tank had to be covered in gravel of certain sizes, to a minimum depth of 8 to 10 cm, graded so that the finest material was on top.

There remained the two problems of determining the precise place where spawning would occur, and the need for a local current. In a trout stream, the female fish selects a gravelly bottom of sufficient depth for her to excavate with her tail a depression into which she deposits her eggs. The water currents however, have to be such that the eggs are directed into the depression and not swept away. We fitted the tank with a false bottom which we covered with a thin layer of gravel, too shallow for spawning except in the centre. Here

43

we cut out an oval shape and made the gravel 8 cm deep in this one spot, adding a large stone to produce a downward current.

Having satisfied all the physical requirements, a pair of fish in breeding condition were placed in the tank, which was illuminated from above and in front. Room lights were extinguished in the hope that we, waiting beyond the lighted area, would be invisible. Not surprisingly, as they had travelled from a fish farm 30 km away, the fish took a couple of days to settle down and become used to their surroundings. Once they had become accustomed to the new environment, however, the female began to dig, by turning on her side and flicking the gravel violently with her tail. At first she worked in the corners, only to encounter the hard base. Soon she concentrated on the place we had chosen. The male fish was in constant attendance; his courtship consisted of nuzzling up to the female and quivering against her. As the excavation became deeper, the female used her anal fin to test the depth and possibly also the size of the

44

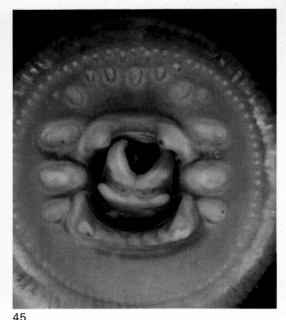

45

44. King John died of a surfeit of lampreys. Nowadays such abundance is seldom found in Britain, but in more than one of the American Great Lakes, relatives of the lamprey once wiped out the entire trout population, until controlled.

45. Equipped with a sucker-like yet jawless mouth, the wickedly abrasive tongue of a lamprey gouges a cruel hole in the host. Body fluids ooze from the wound, to be voraciously lapped up by the parasite.

46. Even the less spectacular film sequences have provided us with food for thought. The black spot on the perch's dorsal fin was clearly used as a shoaling signal between individuals.

46

crevices between pebbles where the eggs would later lodge. The signs were very promising, but since we did not know the time of day or night when spawning might take place we began a 24-hour vigil by rota.

Orgasmic gape

John Paling, our fish specialist, bore the brunt of this project and was naturally keen to be present when the great moment arrived. It happened that he had to attend a formal dinner on the Saturday evening when trout activity was obviously nearing a climax, so Gerald Thompson stood in for him. Throughout the evening, the hen fish continued digging at intervals, and every time she took up a position above her nest or 'redd', the male came alongside and courted her vigorously. Always, however, the hen moved forward before he came level with her nose. Trout spawn side by side, so every time the male came alongside, Gerald reached for the camera button. John returned at 11.30 pm and Gerald stayed on in the hope that

two cameras would be in use that night. Together, Gerald and John sat and waited. At 1.30 am the cock fish swam along the flank of the hen yet again, but this time, she did not move off the redd. As his snout came level with hers, both fish arched their backs, the dorsal fins quivered violently and the mouths gaped wide in an orgasmic release of muscular energy. The eggs were pushed out in a pearly shower into the redd, while a cloud of milky sperm, or milt, enveloped them. Spawning had occurred, and it had lasted only three seconds. The hen moved forward on her side thrashing with her tail so that gravel was flung back to cover the eggs, and she repeated this several times. The cock fish resumed station downstream of the redd. And so the weeks of preparation and days of watching were rewarded by a grandstand view of the most private moments in the life of a trout.

During spawning, some eggs are inevitably washed away and these are readily eaten by other trout in the area. A small proportion of eggs in the redd itself, as well as those which fail to be covered,

47

48

49

50

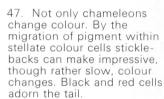

51

47. Not only chameleons change colour. By the migration of pigment within stellate colour cells sticklebacks can make impressive, though rather slow, colour changes. Black and red cells adorn the tail.

48. The intriguing life and times of the stickleback have been the subject of many films. In nesting livery the male fish sports vivid colours and camouflage at the same time.

49. Setting up house takes time and effort. The male stickleback laboriously sucks up gravel and sand into his mouth to create a small depression which he will fill with nest material.

50. A mouthful of sand is not pleasant and it is quickly jettisoned some distance away from the nest site. Time and time again the male stickleback sucks in mouthfuls of sand before transferring them and spitting them out.

51. Plant material is carried into the shallow depression and spat out. The fish then tamps it and finally cements it in place with a kidney secretion.

may be eaten by the dipper, a delightful bird of grace and beauty. The dipper haunts the fast-flowing streams, flying from rock to rock, pushing its head under water and then disappearing beneath the surface to bob up nearby. The brown and white plumage and jaunty tail make the dipper unmistakable above water. Actually joining it in the water where it feeds was another of our exciting filming experiences.

Once again our river tank was pressed into service, this time with a lower water-level and a grassy bank as backdrop. We obtained a permit to enable us to have a dipper netted for study and the wild-caught bird was housed in a cage above the tank, with a ladder leading down to the grass. It settled down immediately, never appearing to be frightened, and it accepted the maggots provided as food during the first night in captivity, whilst it was shut up in the cage. The following morning, we opened the cage door and the bird entered the tank for the first time. At once it flew to a log, put its head under water to look around,

52

53

52. In full courtship colours of iridescent head and back, blue eyes and red belly, the male stickle entices the swollen egg-filled female to the nest.

53. Having pointed to the nest entrance the male withdraws slightly and nuzzles his bride-to-be into position, as if to say, 'In you go, it's your birthday!'

and then jumped neatly into the water. The transformation was amazing. The dumpy brown and white dipper became a sleek bird of silver as the weight of water pressed down the feathers trapping bubbles of air between the barbs. It literally flew to the bottom and began picking up aquatic larvae – 'literally', because the dipper does in fact progress through the water by flying, except that the wings are bent back from the wrist. Presumably the resistance of the water would break a fully-extended wing. After twenty seconds the bird bobbed back to the surface and jumped on the bank. An extended period of elaborate preening followed. In order to keep the body dry, it anoints its feathers with oil from the gland situated at the base of the tail. Like most other aquatic birds, the dipper has a large oil gland.

We sat entranced as the dipper repeatedly entered the water, and we soon saw that if food was not readily apparent it would search for it by picking up stones; which is the way in which it would uncover trout eggs. Later we placed some

minnows in the tank, thinking that these would easily elude the dipper, but to our surprise, the bird caught them without difficulty. It will be a sad day if the delightful dipper ceases to be a feature of our streams and mountain torrents.

It would be a mistake to imply that the brown trout, as a species, suffers predation only in the egg stage and at the hands, or beak, of the dipper. Although the trout is itself a predator and therefore higher up the chain or web of consumer organisms, it falls prey itself to the pike, otter, osprey and also, strangely, from a fish sometimes only one-third its own size. This is the freshwater lamprey, called *Lampetra*, which grips its victims like a limpet and once annihilated the trout from more than one of the American Great Lakes.

The lamprey is a fish with a strange design and even more weird habits. It is jawless, but equipped with a capable sucker and a tongue like a milling cutter which it uses to rasp holes in its host fish. From these holes, body fluids ooze into the rapacious gut of this unpleasant ectoparasite, for that is what the lamprey is. Some of its marine cousins are designed to devour dead or dying fish and dozens may bore their way, head first, into a carcass, filling it with slime and writhing bodies. So deep do these lampreys or 'hagfish' bury their heads, that their respiratory gill slits are channelled back to a common port way down the body. In this way, uncontaminated water can be utilized for respiratory purposes, while head and shoulders burrow into the carcass.

From compost to courtship

The three-spined stickleback is still a relatively common inhabitant of ditches, ponds and certain rivers; in fact it may be found in any place permanently occupied by water. In earlier times it occurred in even greater abundance, and was caught in vast numbers to be spread on the land as manure or rendered down to provide oil for illumination. Rarely exceeding 50 mm, both sexes are similar in appearance during winter – sporting green or brown colouration above, with silvery sides and belly. It is in spring that the males don their breeding colours and appear in their full glory. Then they shine with a tropical splendour among the other fish of lakes and streams. The eyes become a brilliant blue, the breast and throat are a fiery red, as is the lining of the mouth, while the back and sides assume a banded pattern which intensifies in moments of excitement. These colour changes are effected by pigment cells which contract or expand pigment under nervous control.

In spring the mature males leave the shoal, with which they spent the winter, and each seeks a small territory of a square metre or so in shallow water. Rivalry between males is intense and invisible boundaries between adjacent territories result from numerous 'border incidents' where neighbours clash with mouth and spines. Having secured a living space for himself, the male selects a spot on the sandy or muddy bottom. Here he excavates a depression by sucking up mouthfuls of material which he ejects some way from the nest. He lines the depression with strands of delicate weed and algae, prodding them into place with his snout, and cementing them together with

54

55

54. As soon as the female has passed through the nest and released her eggs, the male once or sometimes twice follows suit to liberate his milt or sperm over the eggs.

55. Once fertilized, the eggs develop within the nest. The male keeps them perpetually aerated and free from fungus by fanning movements of his pectoral fins.

56. Like a large fish within a small fish bowl, 8-day-old embryos wriggle and twist. Colour cells, heart, yolk sac, eyes and lenses are all well developed prior to hatching.

57. To one who is 5 mm long, the big wide world must be perplexing and terrifying. At this stage an oil droplet provides buoyancy for the hatchling.

56

57

a secretion from the kidneys. He continues to add more material until the nest projects slightly above the substratum. Finally he pushes his way through the nest to make a tunnel which has an entrance and an exit. The finished nest is about 35 mm in diameter and may be built in a few hours – not allowing for fights with interfering neighbours!

The male now has to wait until a suitable female enters his territory and he occupies the waiting period by continuing to preserve his territorial boundaries, which may expand or contract as a result of combats with neighbours (the boundaries are always flexible). All the time he pays prodding attention to the nest. It is now that the male assumes full courtship colours and his back and head turn to shining, azure blue. The awaited moment arrives when a female, heavy with spawn, as revealed by the grossly swollen belly, swims into the territory. The courtship of most fish is an unromantic, cold-blooded affair, but not so the stickleback's. The swollen body of a gravid female triggers off an elaborate courtship ritual

58. The female *Argulus*, heavy with ripe, white eggs, leaves her host and seeks a sheltered site for egg-laying. Black pigment cells camouflage and protect the otherwise obvious egg mass from ultraviolet light.

59. The frilled suckers, recurved antennal hooks, adhesion pads and body spines of the *Argulus* enable it to hang on to surfaces as smooth and shiny as a fish eye.

60. The freshwater fish louse, *Argulus*, is a common sight to anglers. Feeding as it does upon the body fluids of fish, its presence must be less than welcome.

which can be observed by anyone who keeps sticklebacks in a suitable small aquarium.

Simple experiments soon reveal, however, that a male stickleback does not react to a female fish as such, but only to the swollen shape. A pear-shaped piece of lead, dangled on the end of a thread, will evoke just as strong a courtship response as will the live fish! Behaviourists refer to this as the 'sex bomb'. Curiously, this experiment totally failed when in 1973 we tried to put it on film. Seven years previously it had worked well.

When the male stickleback sights the ripe female, his first act is to creep through the tunnel of his nest, presumably to ensure that the way is clear for his bride. He then begins his rapid zig-zag courtship 'dance', approaching the female in a series of jerks with acute changes of angle between them. As he draws close to her, he jerks and turns back towards the nest. If prepared to spawn, the female swims in a head-up position near the water surface. At first she often appears indifferent to her suitor, and the male may even

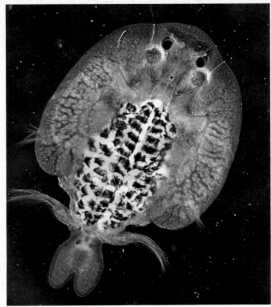
58

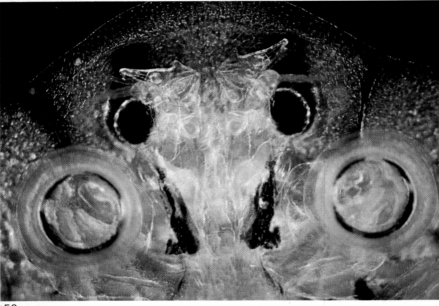
59

60

attack her in what appears to us to be frustration. But sooner or later she suddenly dips head downwards and follows the male to the nest. He now indicates the entrance to her by inserting his snout into it and then turning on his side with his back and spines towards the female. At this stage the female sometimes appears to take fright and returns to the water surface, whereupon the male again begins to court her vigorously. When the female goes to the nest entrance, and begins to force her way into the frail structure, the male backs off. The female, being so much fatter than the male, often damages the nest as she thrusts forward with vigorous tail movements until positioned with her head at the exit and her vent just inside the entrance. The male now switches to a new kind of behaviour; he touches the base of the female's tail with his snout and quivers violently, applying, as it were, a 'vibro-massage'. Slowly her tail begins to rise, a sign that spawning is imminent. When the tail is raised on high, a stream of eggs, fifty to a hundred in number, is quickly released

and, instantaneously, with a violent movement of the tail, the female leaves the nest. Immediately the male follows his mate through the nest and, without stopping, squirts his sperm over the batch of eggs, which are thus fertilized *in situ*. As he leaves his nest, he sees a deflated gaunt fish, his erstwhile spouse, nearby, but as there is now no swelling to arouse his sexual instincts, he chases her out of his territory. If other ripe females approach the male, he may repeat the courtship ritual until his nest is full of eggs.

The female takes no part in caring for the eggs or young. Instead she returns to the shoal and ripens another clutch of eggs which will be deposited in another male's nest. So care of the eggs and young is the sole responsibility of the father, who displays complete devotion to his task. The eggs require a constant source of fresh oxygen and, to this end, the male periodically fans a current of water with his pectoral fins into the entrance of the nest. As the embryos develop the male spends an increasing amount of time at this chore. He also continues

61

to guard his territory and particularly the nest itself – chasing, or in some cases, carrying other animals away. Even a newt, which is considerably larger than a stickleback, will not withstand the onslaught of a stickleback defending its nest.

At first the eggs are almost clear, but by the fifth day the large dark eyes, the beating heart, the ear otoliths and the tail coiled round the embryo can be distinguished through the egg membrane. About this time the male may add sand to the nest, but near the ninth day, when hatching occurs, he begins to suck all the sand out of the nest, and also to tease it apart, so that the young stickles are born into an open network of weed amongst which they can swim without leaving the nest. The newly-born stickle has a large yolk sac protruding from the belly and this provides nourishment for the first day or two, which it mostly spends lying at the bottom of the nest. Once the yolk sac has been absorbed, the stickles must feed themselves and therefore be more active. So far, the swim bladder has been empty of

air and the young fish sink, but the time has come to assume neutral buoyancy, which obviously greatly facilitates swimming. To this end, each baby must make a quick dash to the surface to gulp air for charging the swim bladder. To do this however, they have to elude father who is still guarding the nest against all comers. If he can, the male will catch his young in his mouth as they head for the surface. He has no intention of harming them – instead he carefully spits them back into the nest. It is a rather astonishing fact of nature that while sticklebacks will eat other sticklebacks, the father never eats his own young. I once tried the experiment of dropping mosquito larvae singly from a pipette poked through the water surface immediately above a nest containing young. The male gulped the larvae down without hesitation, but when I released one of his babies in place of a mosquito, he always returned it to the nest.

There are plenty of hazards around however – young stickles are preyed upon by a variety of aquatic adults and larvae, including fish such as

61. Predating the engineer's diving bell by a million or more years *Argyroneta*, the water spider, lives, hunts and breeds under water. Food varies from small fish to surface-struggling insects.

33

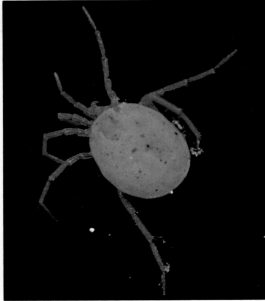

62

63

64

65

62. *Dolomedes*, the raft spider, is found in the sphagnum peat bogs of Ireland. This big wolf spider, perhaps best termed the swamp spider, has exhibited hitherto unknown behaviour before our cameras.

63. Brilliant red swimming mites, *Hydrarachna*, sometimes abound in stagnant ponds. They are curious creatures that spend part of their lives on aquatic insects, as ectoparasitic larvae, and part as free-living adults.

64. *Corixa*'s comical semaphor-like cleaning activity and manipulation of air has provided us with more laughs than we can remember. *Corixa* is otherwise known as the front-swimming water-boatman.

65. The big blue *Aeshnid* dragonflies may spend three years as feeding, developing, aquatic nymphs. Equipped with prehensile mask and wicked jaws, nymphs despatch considerable numbers of aquatic invertebrates, including *Asellus*.

the bullhead and, indeed, other sticklebacks. *Dytiscus* adults and larvae, the nymphs of dragonflies and the unique water spider, all include sticklebacks in their menu. While they remain in and around the nest, the father defends them against all such threats. The stickles feed at first on minute organisms; as they grow, they take increasingly larger food, such as *Daphnia*.

As the days go by, the father's bright colours begin to fade and his protective instincts begin to wane until, about ten days after hatching, the young begin to disperse, and he allows them to do so. Up to this time the young have shown no sign of the three dorsal spines and the two pelvic spines which play such a prominent part in the fighting, display and defence of adult fish. The spines begin to appear about the time the young leave the nest and they serve as a very real defence against many would-be predators. The important factor in the saga of 'eat and be eaten' is the relative size of predator and prey. The spines of the adult stickle obviously constitute protection against a wider range of predators in terms of size than those of the baby stickle. But predators above a certain size can ignore the spines of any stickleback. This is well shown by the largest predator of fresh water, the pike, discussed earlier. Large pike do not catch very small prey unless they are exceedingly hungry, in which case a stickleback will be swallowed like a pill. Baby pike of 75 to 100 mm find the spine of young stickles too much for comfort, and larger pike are defeated by the adults and soon learn to avoid them.

When a stickleback is taken into the mouth of a pike, it erects the dorsal and ventral spines which catch in both the tongue and the lining of the mouth. The pike appears to suffer considerable discomfort as it shakes its head and opens its mouth. Eventually the stickleback will be spat out to swim away unharmed. Its spines, however, offer no protection against a more insidious enemy, the fish louse, *Argulus foliaceous*. This small crustacean is found on the skin of almost all species of freshwater fish. It is a temporary parasite which swims from host to host to feed.

66

Argulus has been known for over 300 years as a serious enemy of freshwater fishes, and although, from early times, investigators have studied it in great detail, a successful way of dealing with the parasite in nature has not been found.

Argulus is beautifully adapted to a parasitic way of life. The dorso-ventrally flattened shape gives minimum resistance as its host swims through the water. The body is so transparent that wherever it attaches itself to the host, it remains almost invisible. For clinging to the smooth scales of a fish, it has two large suckers, each with a rim which serves as a seal; these can be moved independently so that the parasite can 'walk' over the host's body. There are also numerous small backward-directed spines around the head and over the ventral surface of the body and limbs.

When *Argulus* lands on a fish it provokes a violent reaction. This results from the insertion into the host of a hollow spine to which a poison sac is attached. Poisonous anticoagulant is injected into the fish's blood stream, where it breaks down the walls of the blood cells. The liquefied blood can then be sucked up by a pumping action of the pharynx, which is housed within a vacuum-like proboscis, situated behind the poison spine. A heavily infected fish develops a characteristic pallor because the *Argulus* poison breaks down not only the blood cells but also the colour cells. Fish of all sizes are often killed by the fish louse. Free-swimming *Argulus* are readily seized by sticklebacks as food, but the efforts of the fish to swallow the parasite are defeated by *Argulus* hanging on with its suckers and spines inside the mouth of the fish until eventually, as in the case of the pike and stickleback, the 'food' is ejected alive and unharmed. This intriguing last-resort behaviour by *Argulus* we came upon while filming.

Less frequent enemies of sticklebacks are two unrelated kinds of spider. *Argyroneta aquatica*, the water spider, is unique in spending the whole of its life under the surface of water, although it can, if necessary, travel over land from one body of water to another. Like all other spiders the water

66. The hog-louse, *Asellus* – a ubiquitous scavenger – attains tremendous population numbers in the late summer and autumn when the summer flux of animal and plant growth wanes.

35

67. The ramshorn snail's connection with sheep is not confined to its appearance. Closely related species also harbour the parasitic larvae of the sheep liver fluke flatworm — the causative agent of sheep liver rot.

68. With a tongue like a coiled precision-milling cutter, the ramshorn snail spends a life-time rasping plant and rock surfaces free of algal slimes and encrustations.

69. The larva of *Dytiscus*, the great diving beetle, has broadly spaced, hollow, recurved jaws which are a challenge to most fresh-water invertebrates. Anti-coagulant is pumped into the victim and body fluids sucked out.

67

68

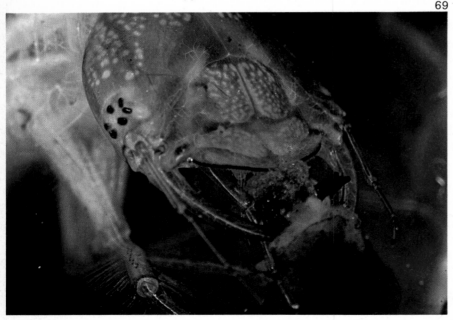

69

spider breathes free air, and does not, as do many aquatic animals, make use of oxygen dissolved in the water. This means that the spider is quite independent of the oxygen level in the water. However, in practice it can only live in water which contains sufficient oxygen to support the animals that it requires as food, and therefore it will not be found in stagnant places.

The water spider, *Argyroneta*, lives in an underwater home which it starts by weaving a curved silken platform attached to plants. Then it climbs up adjacent plants, or swims upwards until its front legs touch the surface film, whereupon the abdomen is jerked downwards while the hind legs are stretched out to encompass a bubble of air. A sudden jerk of body and legs traps a large bubble between the hind legs and the spider uses the remaining three pairs of legs to paddle home. It approaches the platform from below, head uppermost, and the bubble, which was trailing behind, passes forward; the hind legs may be used to stroke it and at once the platform becomes more convex. More silk is added, between visits to the surface for air, and soon a sort of improvised diving bell is formed — shining like silver with the air it contains. The spider shelters, feeds, moults, mates and lays eggs inside her home, replacing the air from time to time. The water spider is a hunter, feeding on aquatic insects and the fry of fish: young sticklebacks may be caught if they approach too close, and insects falling on the water surface are seized from below in an instant. As she moves in her element air trapped among the hairs of the velvety abdomen makes her shine like silver.

A spider that fishes
The other spider, *Dolomedes*, will readily climb below the water surface to hide when alarmed. But she is more usually seen sitting beside a stream or pond with her front legs resting on the water surface. Her chocolate-brown body is handsomely ornamented by a white or yellow stripe along each side. This spider feeds mainly on insects which have fallen on the water and which have become entrapped in the surface film. Their struggles set up ripples which the spider detects through her legs. A quick dash across the water surface, trailing a silken thread attached to her perch, results in the prey being seized and taken back to base to be eaten at leisure.

While filming this spider recently, we observed it behaving in a way which appears not to have been recorded before. The spider was sitting on water weed beside a small pool containing young fish about 15 mm long. Suddenly we noticed that one of the fish was swimming near the spider, which in turn immediately started dappling the water surface by disturbing it rapidly with the tarsus of one front leg. The fish was attracted to the movement, possibly mistaking the ripples for those created by a small struggling insect. As it came within range, the spider lunged at the fish and disappeared beneath the surface in a cloud of spray, only to reappear almost at once with the fish firmly grasped. At first we were sceptical that the spider had intentionally 'fished', using a method very similar to anglers who dap a fly on the surface to catch dace. Subsequently, however, we wit-

70

71

72

70. The home of the Trinidadian bromeliad frog, *Amphodus*, is no larger than an egg cup. It lives, feeds and breeds in the water-filled centres of epiphytic bromeliads found in upland rain forests.

71. *Amphodus* has developed the gymnastic ability to leap accurately backwards and downwards, so it can retreat into its watery home. Its flattened profile then permits it to back deeply into the bromeliad leaf spaces.

72. The smaller the family, the more demanding the care required. *Nototheca*, the Trinidadian marsupial frog, lays two precious eggs only, and helped by the male, transfers the eggs to an incubation pouch on her back.

nessed similar behaviour by *Dolomedes* several times. Often it was successful; on other occasions the fish avoided capture. We are now convinced that *Dolomedes* is an occasional angler, and the cine film we made adds weight to this.

Many organisms within the pond community are familiar to layman and specialist alike. A child's net, scooped through the underwater vegetation and debris of a pond in high summer seldom fails to capture such things as red swimming mites, back and front swimmers – *Notonecta* and *Corixa* respectively, hog lice, *Asellus*, dragonfly nymphs, pond snails and dytiscid water beetle larvae. All associate directly or indirectly with one another. All transfer what was originally solar energy, harnessed by aquatic plants, one stage further along and up the food web. All are admirably suited to their particular niche in life. All have unknowingly intrigued children and adults since man first took notice of his aquatic surroundings. All have featured as captivating subjects before OSF cameras and all have provided us, at least, with

one hitherto unknown fact about themselves.

Until we had filmed them we never realized that corixid front swimmers feed actually beneath mud and debris, and differ so markedly in their behaviour from their back-swimming cousins. We never realized hog lice virtually disappear during high summer and only explode their population numbers in the autumnal freshwater rot! We were not aware that dragonfly nymphs, once swallowed by American blue-gills, are rapidly spat out because of their vicious anal spines. After one such encounter the blue-gill in question turned upside down and died, but for just what reason death occurred we do not know. We had no idea either how miracidial sheep liver fluke larvae entered their ramshorn snail (*Limnea truncatula*) hosts, until we watched and photographed them swim up to the expanded foot of the snail, where they appeared to slough their cilia and burrow straight into the foot tissue.

So far, our 'unseen' freshwater examples have hailed from northern temperate regions, but there

73. This miraculous, diminutive, yellow-flowered death-trap called *Utricularia*, the bladderwort, is seldom noticed, but often present in northern hemisphere ponds and lakes.

74. *Utricularia*'s capture of water-fleas and mosquito larvae is akin to the workings of a piece of precision engineering. It is triggered, opens, sucks and closes in less than 1/700th of a second.

75. Victims are not always completely engulfed by the bladderwort's firing. *Daphnia* may be caught by antennal hairs and mosquito larvae may be caught by siphon bristles alone.

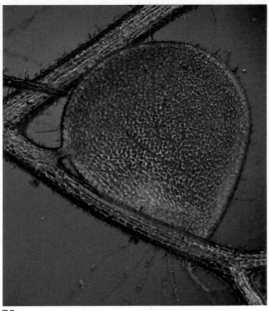

73

74

76. Mosquito larvae are amazing creatures in their own right. The phantom midge, *Chaoborus*, has a larva capable of motionless, mid-water buoyancy and split-second reversal of position.

77. Situated just behind the compound eye of *Chaoborus* is a single ocellus. The function and origin of this apparently misplaced facet are mysteries.

its tadpoles are only found in bromeliads on the very tip of El Tucuche, a 900-metre-high mountain cloaked in misty rain forest in the North Mountain Range of Trinidad. Attempts to locate *Amphodus* elsewhere in South America have drawn a blank. The frog remains an enigma. Perhaps *Amphodus* chose its home with solitude in mind, for it is a gruelling, 6-hour foot-slog against rugged gradient and vegetation from the end of the Maraval Valley to Tucuche's summit. Only an avid *Amphodus*-hunter is likely to go to such trouble!

Frogs and bladderworts

Amphodus, probably isolated on its mountain top since the end of the last glaciation, some 20,000 years ago, is perfectly adapted to brome-liad life. It is dorso-ventrally flattened, so that it can squeeze down between the leaf-bases when startled – indeed, it is possibly unique in being the only frog that jumps backwards. As a member of the group of frogs called the Hylidae – tree frogs – *Amphodus* has sucker-discs on its fingers and toes, enabling it to clamber over damp and slippery leaf surfaces. *Amphodus* feeds on small insects – mosquitoes, termites, and flies – and lays its eggs in the bromeliad-pools. The tadpoles feed upon a rich soup of rotting organic matter and algae. They are almost devoid of external colouring, since they need no protection against the damaging effects of ultra-violet light, precious little of which filters into their murky world. If a tadpole is decanted into clear water, its blood system and digestive tract are displayed as clearly as in a plexiglass laboratory model.

Amphodus tadpoles are virtually immune from predation in their isolated bromeliad pools. Other amphibia suffer terrible attrition in the tadpole stage, which is the reason for the vast numbers of eggs produced. *Amphodus*, however, is not alone in producing a small number of well-protected tadpoles. By carrying two eggs in a pouch on her back, *Nototheca fitzgeraldi*, the marsupial frog, literally guards them with her life.

Moreover, the whole tadpole stage goes on inside the egg, which hatches directly into a minia-ture froglet. To satisfy the nutritional requirements of the imprisoned tadpoles, which in most amphibia spend several weeks voraciously feeding on algae and water plants, *Nototheca*'s eggs are huge, and laden with yolk – which provides the tadpoles' nutritional needs. In this case, nature has ensured survival of the species by offering protection in size rather than in the necessity of laying thousands of small eggs.

Returning now to temperate climes yet to no less spectacular an organism, there is an under-water plant that traps and digests animals. It may sound like a science-fiction invention, yet the bladderwort, *Utricularia*, with its frail yellow flowers above the surface, and delicate branching stems below, is found to do just that on close inspection. Whilst taking its place alongside the other members of the pond plant-community, as generators of oxygen, and a source of food for herbivores, the bladderwort has evolved an amazing facility for supplementing the supply of nutrients acquired by its root system. It literally devours small aquatic insect larvae and crustacea.

are other equally amazing, exciting-to-witness examples of unseen adaptation and behaviour taking place in foreign parts.

A cupful of murky water trapped in the leaves of a bromeliad might seem a poor choice of home. However, the water held in bromeliads – epiphytes commonly found in tropical rain forest – provide a constant and static freshwater environment colonized by a whole gamut of organisms. These range from protozoa to amphibia, various species of which spend either the whole, or part, of their life cycles in these countless miniature ponds. Some animals, like mosquitoes, merely inhabit brome-liad water during their larval life. Others, such as scorpions, use bromeliads as a damp hiding-place from which to forage for prey, and could as easily take up residence elsewhere. Still others are as wedded to bromeliad life as camels to the desert, and are found nowhere else.

Amphodus auratus, the bromeliad frog, is a case in point which has taken this dependency seemingly to the point of absurdity. For *Amphodus* and

Arranged at 3-mm intervals along its underwater stems are miniature 'blunder-traps', which perform the double function of mouth and stomach. Each trap, or bladder, is a hollow, 1.5-mm-long chamber attached to the stem by a stalk, and equipped with a hinged trapdoor. To 'set' the bladder, a metabolic pump slowly evacuates its fluid contents, and because the trapdoor is tightly shut, the sides of the bladder collapse inwards, thus taking on a lean and hollow-cheeked appearance. Around the trapdoor is an array of guide-hairs, the function of which is to funnel an approaching animal towards the door and its minute trigger-hairs. If a trigger-hair is touched, the trapdoor is released and flies open inwards; water rushes in as the walls of the bladder spring outwards. The hapless prey is carried into the bladder by the miniature tidal wave, and the trapdoor slams shut behind it. The whole trapping operation is over in 1/700th of a second. The metabolic pump then resets the bladder, and digestive enzymes are released in small quantities to digest the prey.

75

Buoyant phantom

A successful bladder eventually becomes so clogged with the remains of its victims that it is unable to operate, its function being taken over by new bladders on the growing stem. By the end of the summer season a bladderwort plant may be clogged with food-stuffed bladders. So little fresh growth occurs to replace the defunct traps that the plant appears black rather than green.

A mosquito larva that would seldom, if ever, be trapped by *Utricularia* is the larva of *Chaoborus*, the phantom midge. The larva is one of those pond inhabitants that seems to 'disappear' for years at a time; then one day a collecting net will surface with dozens of the glass-like larvae writhing in the bottom. The most remarkable feature of these larvae is that they can adjust their buoyancy perfectly. They can lie in mid-water, absolutely motionless, and this they do while lying in wait for water-fleas and small nymphs and larvae of insects, which they grab with paired semi-raptorial limbs. The buoyancy chaoborids achieve results from controlling the gas-content of two anterior and two posterior swim bladders. Being gas-filled, these bladders are very silvery under water, although melanophores, or black pigment cells, partly cover the top surfaces of the bladders. A similar adaptation occurs in certain deep-sea creatures, and is believed to enhance mid-water camouflage. The fact that it frequents mid-water is what keeps *Chaoborus* safe from capture by the bladderwort. A final adaptation that *Chaoborus* has developed is the ability to flex its sinuous body into a half-hitch, and by this action, totally reverse its position in the water.

For these and various other reasons it has always struck us that phantom midge larvae are amongst the most highly adapted aquatic inhabitants of ponds and other standing bodies of fresh water. The degree of sophistication of this animal to its environment matches the extreme adaptations that we shall now start to consider in that much older and more consistent environment, the sea.

76

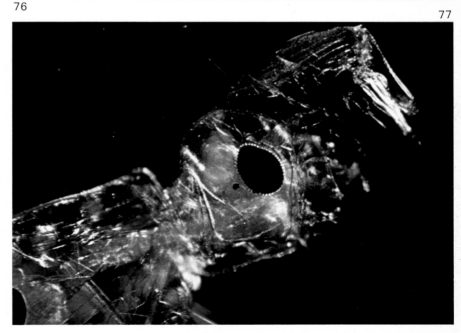

77

39

Chapter 3

The Seashore World

From the confines of fresh water we now turn to the immeasurably larger and more diverse world of the sea. Covering more than two thirds of the earth's surface, the sea provides a richer and infinitely larger arena for life than we, as terrestrial beings, generally appreciate. Our environment is essentially two-dimensional and, despite remarkable adaptive radiation and specialization in some groups, is nevertheless congenial to representatives of only one fifth of the major divisions or phyla of the animal kingdom. In contrast the sea, which is the cradle of life and hence inhabited far longer, provides, or at some time has provided, a three-dimensional environment for members of every known phylum.

The oceans of our planet occupy a staggering 1,346 million cubic kilometres, all of which are available to animal life for exploitation. Although relatively little lives in the cold darkness of the ocean depths – which in several places lie 8 kilometres beneath the surface swell and in the Mindanao Trench in the northern Pacific descend to 11 kilometres – there seems to be no part of the sea that is lifeless. One way of visualizing just how much this enormous volume of inhabitable space amounts to is to consider the depth of water that would cover the earth's surface if the land masses were spread smoothly, joined together without mountains or valleys. If such were the case, the waters of the oceans would cover the globe uniformly to a depth of 3,600 metres.

In this chapter, however, we shall confine ourselves to the prolific, but largely unseen, animal life that inhabits the seashore. Watching waves breaking on the shore in a narrow band of foam, it is easy to imagine that this turbulent fringe of the sea is a simple and sparsely populated zone, shunned by marine and terrestrial creatures alike. Nothing could be further from the truth! This no-man's-land between the tides, exposed alternately to the heat of the sun and the pounding of the surf, is inhabited by a fauna of extraordinary diversity and richness. In fact it is a classic example of the principle that the greatest number of niches, and hence number of species, is to be found where different habitats adjoin. Thus the margin of field or forest supports a greater faunal diversity than the centre, and so it is with the seashore. In addition, the seashore supports large populations of many of its inhabitants, which in

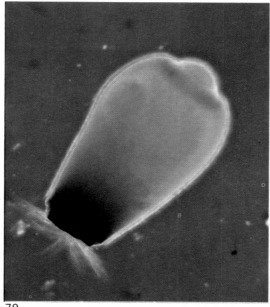

79

78. Ghost crab blowing bubbles.

79. Nothing looks more like an orbiting space capsule equipped with booster rocket and heat shield than the ciliated planula larva of sponges. Plankton hauls south of Melbourne, Australia, took thousands of planulae.

turn reflects a richness in food supply and productivity.

Our understanding of the seashore dates back to 1755, when John Ellis, a London merchant deeply interested in natural history, published his *Essay towards a Natural History of the Corallines, and other Marine Products of Like Kind, commonly found on the Coasts of Great Britain and Ireland.* Following John Ellis's lead came a remarkable stream of amateur naturalists writing with understanding and authority on their chosen groups. Some were gentlemen of leisure with large estates and substantial means but others, exhibiting remarkable determination, laboured under great hardship. Such an example may be seen in Mr Charles Peach, best remembered today for the burrowing sea anemone named in his honour. As a lowly Cornish coastguard in the 1840s, with a wife and nine children to support on four shillings a day, he regularly held members of the British Association for the Advancement of Science spellbound, with accounts of the animals he had newly discovered and observed.

By the middle of the nineteenth century the interest in natural history, and the seashore in particular, had become a national passion in Britain, encouraged by a steady stream of delightful and

80

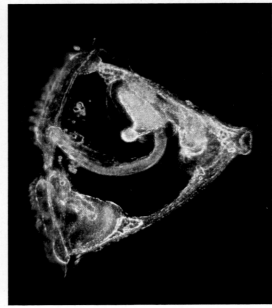

81

80. The thousands of square kilometres that make up the rocky sea bed of inshore waters are carpeted with encrusting sponges. The inhalant/exhalant chambers or paragasters are, in turn, dwellings for many other organisms.

81. Flying wings were scrapped around 1950. The 1/200-mm cyphonautes, 'flying wing' larva of ectoproct moss animalcules, glides on with no fear of redundancy or scrapping.

informative books by authors such as Philip Gosse and Charles Kingsley. To a Victorian audience their books proved doubly acceptable owing to the numerous object lessons in high morality which interspersed the biology. This boom in natural history during the last century is of particular significance to the present conservation-minded and pollution-conscious generation. Before Philip Gosse died, in 1888, he witnessed and understood the disastrous effects that can stem from excessive human interference in natural habitats, even those as apparently rugged and stable as the seashore. We have a fair idea of the irreparable damage that has been done over the past hundred years, but we can only guess at what the future will hold as technological and population pressures continue to increase.

The shore line of the oceans is known as the littoral zone; that is to say, the zone covered by the high spring tides and exposed by the low spring tides. This intermittent exposure to the air is only one of a large number of factors that influence the littoral zone, contributing to its variety and richness. Around the shores of Britain, which with their numerous headlands, and inlets, beaches and mudflats extend for thousands of kilometres, it has been calculated that the littoral zone amounts to some 240,000 hectares. With such an area at his disposal, the alert and enterprising observer can still hope to discover species as yet unknown and witness events as yet unrecorded.

On tropical shores the opportunities are even greater. OSF's first excursion abroad was to Jamaica, where we tried for the first time a newly designed and built periscope system for filming under water. The clear shallow waters of the mangrove swamps near Port Royal proved an ideal testing area and provided a great wealth of strange creatures for our cameras. Schools of little fish clustered around us, attracted by their own reflections in the periscope's glass porthole, and the bed of the lagoon was packed with sedentary jellyfish that lay on their backs with tentacles outstretched above. The greatest prize of all however was a curious little creature called *Berthelinia*. A

gastropod mollusc, *Berthelinia* belongs to a group which, until very recently, was known only as fossils and had long been thought to be extinct. Its most remarkable feature is its hinged bivalve shell – something no other gastropod possesses. In fact *Berthelinia* may truly be called a kind of invertebrate coelacanth, and it was particularly gratifying to be able to record its activities on film for the first time ever.

Shore-line sponging
However, let us first consider a rocky shore. The effects of the rise and fall of the tides are immediately apparent from the horizontal zonation of plant life and, albeit less conspicuously, of animal life down the rocks. Close examination shows that each species maintains a precise and constant relationship with its neighbours. In addition the floral and faunal composition is also affected by the degree of exposure to the force of heavy oceanic breakers as well as by geographical position. This affects the time of day at which low-water springs occur. As it is constant in a given location, it influences the degree of heating and desiccation resulting from the sun's rays. The sea water itself can also vary considerably in temperature, salinity and in the amount of suspended matter it contains. These and many other subtle influences exert a delicate but firm pressure that renders a spot suitable for colonization by one member of a genus, but totally alien for colonization by a close relative.

If we pause to examine a small pool, left amongst the rocks by the ebbing tide, we may be struck at once by the profusion of growths that cover the rock surface, particularly those on the sheltered face of an overhanging boulder. Protected from the direct rays of the sun, a multitude of orange, green and yellow organisms compete for space. In fact these apparently simple plant-like encrustations belong to several quite distinct phyla and span a broad spectrum of complexity and organization. At the lower end of the scale, and perhaps the most abundant, are the sponges.

Some 250 species are known from around the

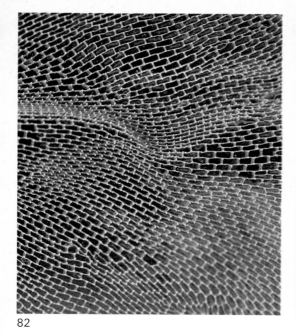

82

83

84

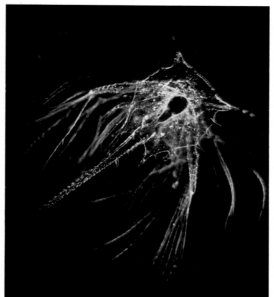

85

82. At a distance, the lattice-work living accommodation for *Membranipora*, a bryozoan ectoproct, resembles a white patch or blemish on the surface of weed.

83. The bryozoan *Flustrella* invariably establishes its tenement 'city' on fronds of a seaweed. When the tide washes in, thousands of cilia-beating, filter-feeding individuals fish the food-rich waters.

84. A colony of goose barnacles hang, bat-like, from beneath a drifting plank. Arms stretched wide, they occasionally sweep the otherwise gently-passing conveyor of micro-organisms for their next meal.

85. Final-stage naupliar larvae of goose-barnacles pirouette with ungainly antennae, which operate like unsynchronized oars. Only in 1830 were nauplii recognized to be young barnacles.

coasts of Britain alone, one of the commonest being the breadcrumb sponge, which is very variable both in shape and colour. None of the British sponges are commercially important like the Mediterranean bath sponge, whose protein-fibre skeleton has been collected and marketed from the earliest times. Indeed, Glaucus, who built the *Argo* in which Jason and his mythical companions sought the Golden Fleece, was by profession a sponge diver. However, it is not surprising to learn that the animal nature of sponges escaped observers for many years. Although Aristotle, who wrote at some length on sponges, considered them intermediate in nature between plants and animals, succeeding generations placed them firmly in the plant kingdom. Even the great Linnaeus, father of modern systematic zoology, held this view. It was not until 1825, when Dr Grant of Edinburgh observed the water currents produced by sponges through his microscope, that their true position was recognized and accepted. Even after this, there were still some who tried to argue

the plant nature of sponges, but they were misled by certain freshwater species which contain symbiotic green algae and produce seed-like reproductive bodies called gemmules. The ultimate proof came with the realization that no sponge contains cellulose, a universal component of plant tissues.

Despite their simplicity sponges are quite remarkable animals. Zoologists place them at the bottom of the classificatory tree as being the simplest multicellular animals. However, this should not be taken to indicate that the sponges have been a stepping-stone to higher forms. Rather the sponges must be regarded as an evolutionary experiment that has been only partially successful – a dead end, as it were, leading to no further elaboration or complexity.

The body of a sponge consists of aggregations of cells arranged in a regular pattern, but differing from all other multicellular creatures in the absence of nervous coordination. The most characteristic cells that make up the sponge body are

86. The seventh-stage barnacle nauplius soon metamorphoses into a curious grappling-hook-equipped Cyprid larva. This bivalved stage seeks a settling site, anchors itself and again metamorphoses into a diminutive barnacle.

87. This serves as a reminder why the final larval stage of a barnacle should be called a Cyprid. The barnacle larva bears a striking resemblance to the fresh and saltwater *Cypris*, a bivalved Ostracod.

called choanocytes or collar cells. They each possess a long flagellum and are arranged in a cup-like pattern. The continual beating of the flagella sets up water currents, which flow into the body, through a series of minute pores over the surface, and leave through common exhalant openings called oscula. These water currents draw in minute particles of organic debris, which are filtered off for food, carry away metabolic wastes, and keep the sponge supplied with dissolved oxygen.

The classification of sponges is complex, and is based upon the nature of the skeleton. This, if present, consists of strands of a protein called spongin or of multi-rayed calcareous or siliceous spicules. For this reason and the very variable nature of a sponge's appearance, depending upon where it is growing, field identification can rarely be made with any degree of certainty.

Sponges are able to reproduce by the simple expedient of budding off small fragments, which then continue to grow and develop into new individuals. Conversely, they are also able to coalesce, so that many large encrustations, like those completely covering the sides of a rock pool, may have originated as a series of discrete and independent sponges. In addition to asexual budding, sponges are also able to reproduce sexually, which is of importance not only in maintaining the plasticity resulting from the mixing of genetic material, but also in helping to distribute the species.

Bryozoa and barnacles

All sessile organisms must possess, at some stage in their life history, a mobile distributive phase. As we shall see later, this phenomenon has become a major feature of marine life and appears to have developed, often quite independently, in almost every phylum. All sponges produce both ova and spermatozoa, but fertilization may be either internal or external. In the former, spermatozoa are carried by inhalant currents into the sponge, where they eventually meet an ovum. This develops into a ciliated embryo which eventually ruptures the cavity in which it has been growing and is carried out by the exhalant current as a mobile, free-living planula larva. After swimming about for some twenty-four hours, wafted by the tides and currents, the planula settles and metamorphoses into a post-larval platelet that still retains limited powers of movement by creeping about like an amoeba. It is from these platelets that the adult sponges eventually grow.

In Australia, a year ago, we encountered thousands of sponge planulae in our plankton hauls. Their bullet-like shape and direct, though changeable, 'flight' makes them look just like miniature spacecraft. This, plus their bright colouration, makes them attractive film subjects, and that was our object in Australia – to make a detailed film about the life and times of shore-line inhabitants.

Amongst the other sessile encrusting organisms inhabiting a rock pool, but far removed from the sponges in their level of organization, are members of the phylum Ectoprocta or Bryozoa. These are colonial creatures, each colony being made up of numerous individuals known as zooids. Some

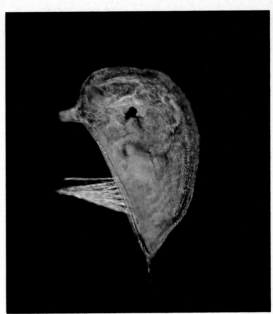

86

87

species grow in flat sheets whilst others form branching colonies that are easily mistaken at first sight for seaweeds. Perhaps the most conspicuous and familiar bryozoan is *Membranipora*, which forms extensive whitish growths on strands of smooth seaweeds such as *Laminaria*. At first sight *Membranipora* appears as a geometrical arrangement of small rectangles fitted together. Each rectangle is the home of an individual zooid and is a secreted, tough, box-like skeleton. The occupant is only to be seen if the colony is carefully observed in still water, free from any vibration. Gradually, from each box, a circlet of delicate tentacles appears, each densely fringed in ciliated cells. These rapidly build up feeding currents to waft small food particles towards the mouth lying within the lophophore, the name given to the ring of tentacles. The true beauty of the extended lophophores of a bryozoan colony are perhaps more readily appreciated in the related genus *Flustrella*. This grows as a nondescript brownish excrescence on the stalks of seaweeds such as the

88

bladderwracks. As the lophophores extend, the whole colony becomes alive as it is enveloped in a pale diaphanous sheen of gently waving twitching tentacles.

The arrangement of the bryozoan body is, as previously noted, far more complex than that of the lowly sponge. In addition to a distinct gut, open at both ends, and a concentrated nervous system, the bryozoan body is constructed around a coelom. This is an internal fluid-filled cavity found only in higher animals. It is totally enclosed and functions, amongst other things, as an hydraulic skeleton. In bryozoans the coelom runs up inside the tentacles of the lophophore. In the contracted condition the tentacles are inverted within the body, rather like the fingers of a glove pulled inside out. The contraction of muscles in the body wall causes the pressure in the coelomic fluid to rise, and the tentacles of the lophophore are everted and extended.

It has already been mentioned that sessile organisms undergo a mobile larval stage for distri-

bution and the selection of a suitable site for the future adult abode. The bryozoans have a highly mobile larval stage that is called a cyphonautes. About the size of a pin point, and hence visible only under the microscope, cyphonautes larvae are very common in the plankton of coastal waters. In essence they consist of a digestive tract contained within a pair of small triangular plates which are kept afloat by a ring of beating cilia. In motion, cyphonautes are reminiscent of flying wings. They are, indeed, very flattened; their triangular shape and the position of their cilia make them hydrodynamically stable, with the apex of the triangle always out in front.

Probably the most painfully obvious inhabitants of the rocky shore, as any grazed child will testify, are the barnacles. Present in enormous numbers, barnacles often excite comment because they are able to establish themselves so far above the mean tide-level, well into the splash zone. In fact they are among the most specialized and the most successful creatures of the shore, although the living

88. Constantly wafting respiratory limbs pump water over the carapace-covered gills of the Bermudan box crab. The water leaves the gill area as a steady fountain, just above the mouth.

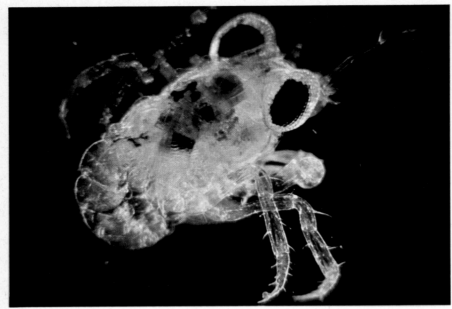

89

90

89. In 1828 Vaughan Thompson discovered that shore crabs begin life as diminutive planktonic larvae. After several zoeal stages the megalops stage precedes settling out.

90. The Bermudan ghost crab, *Ocypode*, has probably supplied OSF with more hilarious filming hours than any other subject. Their speedy tiptoe beach running outpaces the most agile cameraman.

animal itself is seldom observed. The body of a barnacle is profoundly modified in form and strikingly different from that of its near relatives. These modifications are closely linked to the unusual stresses to which barnacles are subjected, most obvious of which is the tremendous pounding of the surf as the breakers hit the shore. Prolonged exposure to the air between tides causes problems of temperature, desiccation and osmotic balance that are more extreme than those usually encountered by marine organisms. There are also difficulties to be overcome in both feeding and reproduction. The great majority of barnacles are hermaphrodite and fertilize one another by means of a long intromittant organ. This ensures a high level of mating success but is, of course, only effective in areas where the individuals are densely packed. Many years ago we unknowingly filmed the intromittant organ in action, but until a year ago we believed it to be a commensal worm inhabiting the calcareous test of the barnacle, and reaching out on a feeding foray!

Not surprisingly, the very modifications and adaptations that have enabled barnacles to flourish in such alien conditions effectively conceal their relationships with other organisms. For this reason barnacles were regarded as molluscs, along with snails and squids, until as recently as 1830. This was only about twelve years before Charles Darwin, best known as the father of evolutionary theory, began work on his classic monograph on the barnacles of the world. The clue to the crustacean affinities of the barnacles, firmly uniting them with crabs, shrimps and waterfleas, was the discovery of their mobile larval stage, by Vaughan Thompson in Ireland in the late 1820s. Like many other crustaceans, barnacles pass a period of their lives as nauplius larvae. After growing and moulting several times, the little dispersive nauplius is transformed into a rather different type of larva called a cypris. This is so named because of its superficial resemblance to seed-shrimps belonging to the genus *Cypris*, members of the crustacean subclass Ostracoda. The cypris larva, which does not feed, at first swims free and seeks a settling site. Then it creeps slowly over the rocks, or boat bottom, upon which it settles, clawing itself along with grappling hooks, to seek a site that will satisfy its requirements as an adult barnacle. When the right conditions are encountered, the larva attaches itself head downwards using special cement glands on the second pair of antennae. Once attached, metamorphosis into the adult form takes place. First, the abdomen is reduced in size and then heavily armoured plates develop to enclose the body. Finally, the legs are transformed into finely fringed fans or cirri that sweep through the surrounding water to filter out edible particles. It is interesting to compare this active feeding of the sessile barnacles with the quite passive use of the cirri in the stalked goose barnacles, which hang from pieces of driftwood or secreted bubble rafts and so move passively about the open ocean.

Parasitic castration

The barnacles' propensity for adaptation reaches its most bizarre expression in some of the parasitic species belonging to the order Rhizocephala. One of the strangest of these is *Sacculina*, which invades the body of a crab. This extraordinary animal starts life as a free-swimming nauplius larva, which provides virtually the only clue to its position in the animal kingdom. In time, the nauplius attaches itself to the body of a suitable crab. Once established on the body of its host it loses its limbs, becoming little more than a small sac of cells. In this form, it penetrates the body of the crab, injecting cells which send roots throughout the animal. Having thus invaded its host and permeated its body, *Sacculina* reappears as a pale swelling beneath the crab's tail, superficially resembling the mass of eggs of a normal crab in berry (carrying eggs). However, one of the effects of parasitism by *Sacculina* is to prevent maturation, resulting in the atrophy of the gonads, and therefore in so-called parasitic castration. Another effect, highly important to the parasite, is the suppression of moulting by the host.

The barnacles are just one of the seven major

91

91. Ghost crabs are perpetual scavengers along the strand line. Once a year they grab at the chance to overpower, drag underground and devour hatchling green turtles.

92. If stressed, or manhandled, ghost crabs bubble from the mouth. This appears to be a defence reaction but it may also be a method of increasing the oxygen content of retained water.

93. *Corystes*, the burrowing or masked crab, is found below low-water mark around British coasts. With only its channel-shaped antennae protruding to the surface of the sandy bottom, *Corystes* enjoys perfect protection.

94

96

95

97

divisions of the Crustacea. The remaining six are no less remarkable, for we are dealing with by far the largest and most diverse phylum of the animal kingdom, the Arthropoda. The insects, with almost a million described species, form the dominant group of terrestrial arthropods, followed by the arachnids and myriapods. Although the insects include a number of forms that have returned secondarily to an aquatic existence, all are air-breathing and fundamentally adapted for life on land. In contrast, the Crustacea are the dominant arthropod class in aquatic environments. Very few crustaceans have invaded the land success-fully, and even the familiar woodlice, which are probably the best example, are highly restricted in their choice of habitats as they cannot survive far from moisture.

Box crabs and ghosts

The higher Crustacea belong to the subclass Malacostraca, of which the Decapoda are the most familiar. These include the shrimps, crabs and lobsters. Crabs, in particular, attract attention along the shore because of their abundance and size, although the largest species, such as the Japanese spider crabs, with a legspan exceeding 2.4 metres, live permanently in deeper water. In fact over 4,000 species of crab have been de-scribed and all have noteworthy or attractive features. The box crabs, also known as 'shame-faced crabs', hide behind their large flattened claws as they lie buried in sand. The claws, which are densely clothed in hairs, hold back the sand and allow a steady stream of water to be drawn in past the mouth and gills, from whence it is squirted out in a small perpetual fountain above the crab's head.

All around the warmer parts of the world, the fiddler crabs make their home in mangrove swamps and other muddy shores. As the tide recedes, these small crabs emerge from their bur-rows in great numbers and signal to one another with their claws, one of which is disproportion-ately enlarged. This signalling is part of an elabor-ate courtship display and varies between species.

98

99

100

101

94. *Orchestia* has one magnificent claw which may be a male sex-linked characteristic and seems to be used in copulation.

95. A grass-green Australian *Caprella* waits with clenched raptorial limbs for passing victims.

96. An Australian idoteid lies motionless while waiting for passing crustacean prey. Capable of standing erect amongst swaying *Zostera* for hours on end, it was even lost during filming.

97. The planktonic larval sergestid prawn is one of the weirdest of all crustacean larvae. Few other animals have eyes so far stuck out on stalks and a body so bedecked with branching processes.

98. The exquisite detail of crustacean design is best seen in larval stages.

99. It is seldom appreciated how different *Crangon*, the shrimp, is to *Leander* the prawn. In a prawn habitat, away from its native sandy haunts, a shrimp gains little from its cryptic colouration.

100. White worms on rocks invariably turn out to be only calcareous tubes of *Hydroides*.

101. When *Hydroides* extends from its tube, its dark red gills, segmented body and lateral spines are readily discerned. Wide-spread tentacles filter organic materials to the mouth.

At OSF we have a particularly soft spot for ghost crabs, which we came to know well when filming on the island of Nonsuch, off the southern shore of Bermuda. At first sight the beaches appear deserted, except for the occasional turnstone picking its way busily along the strand line in search of sandhoppers and other food. However, if one sits quite still for a few minutes, dozens of pairs of stalked telescopic eyes begin to emerge from the surrounding sand. These are the eyes of the ghost crabs, masters of the beach, keeping watch over their domain. Periodically inundated by storms and high tides, the ghost crabs regularly have to rebuild their burrows, which extend for a metre or so beneath the surface. Time after time, the crab carries up clawfuls of sand, and throws them 15 to 30 cm away from the mouth of the burrow. In time a substantial mound develops, which the crab then tamps down, smoothing it carefully with its claws. Eventually when the work is finished it sits at the mouth of its burrow, peering over the ramparts for any signs of movement in its

102

102. Off the south-western Atlantic coasts of Europe a 30-cm starfish, *Marthasterias*, shows itself within the intertidal zone, where it browses upon other echinoderms and rock-clinging molluscs.

103. Only the orange 'asteroid rudiment' of the third stage brachiolarian larvae of starfish will develop into the adult. The larval perambulator is doomed to a stomachless death.

territory. Any intruder, be it another crab, a lizard or an insect, is immediately attacked and dragged back to the burrow to be consumed underground at leisure.

Beaches suitable for ghost crabs are also frequently suited to the needs of green sea turtles. During the breeding season these massive reptiles emerge from the surf by night and lumber painfully to the top of the beach. Here, above the reach of the waves, they excavate a pit some 60 to 90 cm deep in which they proceed to lay their eggs. After burying the eggs, the mother turtle crawls slowly back to the sea and swims off. About three months later the eggs begin to hatch and the baby turtle hatchlings, only about 7 cm long, fight their way up to the surface. Small and vulnerable, they now face the daunting task of reaching the sea. In a wild flurry of beating flippers the hundred or more hatchlings set off across the beach for the welcoming surf. But predators lurk on every side. Birds appear in large numbers to attack them and they also have to run the gauntlet of the ghost

103

104. A purple-tipped sea urchin, *Psammechinus*, turned on its back and viewed closely. Its tube feet, detritus-removing pedicellariae and prehensile spines become like an animated forest, surrounding a fleshy-tipped mouth.

crabs. It is high drama indeed as the turtles are dragged kicking and struggling to the burrows, only occasionally managing to escape. One breathes a sigh of relief for each hatchling that makes it safely to the water, although out of sight beneath the waves still more hazards are waiting. The young turtle swims ceaselessly towards the horizon, which on Nonsuch Island means south. However, before reaching the open ocean there is a barrier of reefs to be negotiated and here amongst the swirling, spray-capped waves, lie menacing barracudas ready to gorge themselves on all the turtles they can find.

Worms for bait and biology

To the sharp-eyed naturalist exploring the sea-shore for the first time, it must seem that there are an inordinate number of marine worms. They certainly provide ample bait for the ranks of anglers that throng any pier. But to the zoologist, the simple cylindrical shape conceals a fascinating array of creatures that represent several quite distinct phyla. At the lower end of the scale, leaving aside the flatworms and various parasitic groups, there are the ribbon worms and proboscis worms. Known to science as nemertines and priapulids, both these phyla consist of un-segmented worms that have no coelom. The ribbon worms are really quite numerous, but are not often seen by the casual observer for they lie in a tightly coiled mass beneath stones. It is well worth exercising the necessary patience and dexterity in trying to unravel one, for a good-sized specimen of *Lineus*, for example, can prove to be a startling 10 metres in length. Its specific name is not *longissimus* for nothing! At the opposite end of the invertebrate hierarchy there are the coelomate acorn worms, sipunculids and phoronids. All these are burrowing forms, only to be found by digging when the tide is out. Though space does not permit us to explore these neglected byways of the invertebrate world in detail, some account can be given of the acorn worms. Until recently they have been regarded as one of the most advanced

105

106

107

groups and closely linked to the subphylum Chordata, to which all the higher animals, including man, belong. Living in a U-shaped burrow in soft mud, the acorn worms possess gill slits and a tough notocord and it is these details of anatomy which were previously believed to be homologous with those of higher animals. We now know that this is not so, and that the similarity is in fact a misleading one. There is evidence, however, particularly in the structure of the mobile tornaria larval stage, that like the echinoderms, the hemichordates – the name by which the acorn worms and their kin are known – lie not far off the main stem of chordate evolution.

Ragworms and tubeworms

Returning to the subject of animals with a worm-like body, by far the largest and most important group are the true worms or annelids. Of these only the polychaetes concern us here for the oligochaetes are mainly terrestrial or found in fresh water, whilst the leeches are predominantly parasitic, albeit on both marine and freshwater hosts. Neither, therefore, forms part of the littoral community. The annelid body plan marks a great step forward in evolution. The combination of a coelomic hydrostatic skeleton and segmentation has allowed the evolution of larger, more mobile and more specialized forms with serial repetition of essential organs such as gonads and nerve ganglia. Ultimately the adaptable annelid body plan gave rise to the arthropods, which have become by far the most successful of all phyla, both in the number of species and number of individuals. The littoral polychaetes certainly give a good indication of how the annelid evolutionary potential has been exploited. On both sandy and rocky shores one finds many free-living or errant polychaetes, such as ragworms or the brilliant green *Eulalia*, which crawls about mussel beds at low tide. However, it is among the sedentary forms that the greatest modifications are to be found.

A walk along any beach or muddy estuarine shore will reveal a multitude of burrows and much evidence of digging. Much of this activity is the work of sedentary polychaetes, including the lugworm, which is extensively dug for bait by anglers. Digging in sand between the tides, the lugworm is typical of many specialized burrowing species. A primary requirement is the ability to withstand, or at least mitigate, the adverse effects of temperature and salinity changes, and this is done both behaviourally and physiologically. The lugworm, *Arenicola*, constructs an L-shaped tube, open at the surface, and lies head down within it. Sand and organic matter are ingested together, the indigestible material being discharged in little heaps around the open end of the burrow. Above the point where the mouth is busy working, there is a gradual downward movement of the sand resulting in the formation of a small depression some 150 mm from the open end of the L. Safe underground, *Arenicola* is well protected from desiccation and extremes of temperature, but at the expense of a ready supply of oxygen. To overcome this difficulty, the blood of *Arenicola* is rich in haemoglobin, which enables it to extract sufficient for its needs through the frilly gills lying along

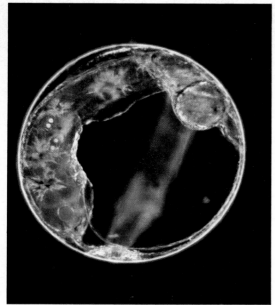

108

109

110

either side of the middle portion of its body, even when there is very little present in the water of the burrow. Many other polychaetes, inhabiting oxygen deficient habitats, also possess haemoglobin in their blood. For example *Cirratulus* and *Amphitrite* inhabit muddy sand, fouled by rotting algal debris, where oxygen is in short supply and an open burrow is impossible to maintain. These worms possess long, brightly-coloured respiratory tentacles which lie on the surface, interspersed with longer feeding tentacles that radiate out from the mouth to trap small food particles. Other worms construct permanent tubes in which to live, either secreting mucus or, as in the case of the sandmason and the peacock worms, for example, sticking sand grains or shell particles together. These species feed by filtering food particles from the surrounding water with their long, ciliated tentacles.

Yet another important and varied group of polychaetes are those that secrete a tough calcareous tube in which to live, like *Hydroides*,

Serpula and *Pomatoceros*. Although the tubes themselves are a common sight as an encrusting growth on rocks, shells and seaweeds, the worms themselves are not often seen, for they only extend their tentacles when covered by the tide, and are very sensitive to disturbance. In an aquarium tank, even the slightest vibration will cause them to withdraw.

Sea potatoes and cucumbers

Not all the signs of animal activity on a sandy beach are the result of worm activity however. Often a small, irregular hole will indicate the presence of something much larger lurking beneath, namely a sand urchin or sea potato. *Echinocardium*, as this creature is called, belongs to the large and wholly marine phylum Echinodermata, which is one of the most advanced invertebrate groups. Indeed, there is strong evidence of evolutionary affinities between the echinoderms and the ancestral vertebrate stock from whence man himself is descended. The fossil record is extremely rich in echinoderm remains, indicating that in times past, there existed a much more diverse fauna than we find today. Living echinoderms fall into five major divisions or classes, of which four (the starfishes, brittlestars, urchins and sea cucumbers) may be found along the seashore. The fifth class, the feather stars or crinoids, are the most primitive and are only to be found in deeper waters. The most striking feature of the echinoderms is the radial symmetry of their bodies, based on a five-part or pentamerous plan. Although there may be further subdivision, as in some starfish with numerous arms, the fundamental arrangement is pentamerous. The body is supported and protected by calcareous plates which interlock to form a ridged armour plating with protruding spines. The sea cucumbers or holothurians are an exception, however, as the plates are reduced to small spicules embedded in the skin. In most species of echinoid these plates are perfect, whole crystals of calcium carbonate.

The other most characteristic feature of the echinoderms is the possession of a water vascular

105. Radiating from around the ventral mouth, the pentamerous red-tipped respiratory tube feet of *Psammechinus* contrast with the sucker-tipped tube feet whose manoeuvrability results from muscle hydraulics.

106. The pearl fish or the fierasfer, *Carapus* must be a candidate for the seven wonders of the natural world. This elongate fish chooses to live in the anal respiratory trees of sea cucumbers!

107. Like many flatfish *Pleuronectes*, the plaice, in early development was not flat. When the larval fish settles out a strange 'face lift' and 'eye twist' takes place.

108. Some fish produce sinking eggs, others like *Pleuronectes* lay pelagic eggs. Eyes, heart, otoliths and yolk sac are all developed after ten days.

109. Dogfish are direct cousins to the larger sharks. All have cartilaginous skeletons and all sink unless they actively swim. Many give birth to live young.

110. The horny mermaids' purses on the strand line are the egg cases belonging to the skate and dogfish family. Sometimes, detached and stranded by storm action, the embryo within remains alive for days.

111

112

system, open to the outside through the madreporite or pore plate on the upper surface. This system provides hydraulic pressure to myriads of tube feet bearing terminal suckers, which provide a slow but steady mobility to the animal. In the case of starfish, which feed upon mussels, the tube feet also provide a means of holding on to the victim's shell. By enveloping the mussel and applying a steady, powerful pull to the two shells, they are gradually eased apart until the starfish is able to insert its protrusible mouth through the narrow gap. It then begins to feed, so weakening the mussel still further, until, eventually, it can offer no resistance.

Pedicellariae and pearl fish
Close examination of the surface of a sea urchin will reveal that spines and tube feet are not the only structures present. Around the mouth, in the middle of the undersurface, is a ring of gills. These delicate, highly branched outgrowths of the body wall are structurally related to other projecting organs, the pedicellariae. Pedicellariae are tentacle-like objects that may be seen in amongst the spines, continuously moving about. Unlike the tube feet, however, they do not end in suckers but in three small jaws each resembling the beak of a bird. In some pedicellariae the jaws contain poison glands and help in defence against predators. Other pedicellariae seem to be used to grasp small prey animals, whilst a third type are specialized for removing any debris that may accumulate on the surface of the urchin, including the settling larvae of other shore-line organisms. This forest of urchin appendages is often the homestead of scale worms and small specialized bivalves.

At first sight, there appears to be little similarity between the sea cucumbers and the other echinoderms, for the body is elongate with openings at each end, giving rise to a secondary superficial bilateral symmetry. In addition there are neither spines nor pedicellariae. However, more detailed examination reveals the presence of a water vascular system, with associated tube feet, and an underlying pentamerous symmetry as well as other typical echinoderm features. Not least of these is the structure of the auricularian larva, of which more will be said later.

The animal kingdom abounds with curious and remarkable associations between species. At OSF we have the good fortune to observe and study many such phenomena and one of the most noteworthy that we have witnessed is that between a sea cucumber and the pearl fish or the fierasfer, *Carapus*. Originally thought to be a symbiotic or commensal relationship in which neither partner suffered (or indeed each mutually benefited), it is now recognised that for part of its life the fish is parasitic on the sea cucumber and totally dependent upon its host. The young fish are free-swimming members of the plankton and are sometimes captured around Britain. Eventually, as the fish grows, it is forced to seek out a sea cucumber of the right species, enter it, head first, through the anus and take up residence in its respiratory trees. At this point it becomes parasitic and feeds on its host's gonads; it is thereafter

113

unable to survive without this food and protection until its maturity. Once it is mature, the fish becomes less dependent upon the sea cucumber and makes frequent excursions outside to feed, although it always returns, now tail first, for protection.

Pearl fish, mudskippers and lumpsuckers

Pearl fish are about 12 cm long, very slender and quite transparent. They are found in many parts of the world, but OSF have had the excitement of finding and filming them only once. In 1967, whilst we were still based in the zoology and forestry departments of the University of Oxford, we decided to spend the summer in Jamaica, testing filming equipment and techniques under expedition conditions. Swimming in the clear, shallow waters that surround the cays lying outside the harbour at Kingston, we soon became adept at spotting the large, reddish-brown species of *Actinopygia* that the pearl fish, *Carapus bermudensis*, occupied. As the sea cucumbers lay on the gleaming white sandy bottom it was not possible to tell whether our quarry lay within, but we soon learnt the simplest way to determine which were inhabited. If placed in a bucket on board our boat, the fish would soon be encouraged by the rise in water temperature to emerge and swim free, probably because of a reduction in oxygen tension. This had the great advantage of not damaging the host cucumbers. It was not unusual to find several fish inhabiting a single individual and once they were returned to cool, fresh sea water they would promptly re-enter their hosts. This they did by approaching the anus of the sea cucumber, head first, and gently tapping. The immediate effect was for the cucumber to close up tight but eventually, as its respiratory needs grew more desperate, it would be forced to give a great sigh and change the water in its respiratory trees, which connect with the cloaca. At this moment the fish would flip its tail round and in an instant slip backwards into the body of its host.

The pearl fish, although living in coastal shallows, is not strictly a member of the seashore community. The prize for the fish best adapted to life between the tides must surely go to the mudskipper, *Periophthalmus*. This delightful creature is an inhabitant of tropical shores and is so well adapted to moving about on mudflats, breathing air, that it is liable to drown if submerged for prolonged periods. Temperate shores harbour nothing as exotic as the mudskipper with its periscopic, bifocal eyes, but nevertheless there are many species that exhibit special adaptations to life in tidepools and coastal waters, where turbulence, temperature and oxygen deficiency are particular problems. The blennies, for example, are covered in slime and have no scales. They respire as much through their skin and fin surfaces as through their gills, and they feed on barnacles and bivalves, biting them off the rock with their powerful jaws. At least one species is known to leave the water from time to time at low tide and bask in the sun. Another species is viviparous, the young being retained within the female body for three months after hatching. This habit, most unusual for fish, saves the young from the hazards of a planktonic

114

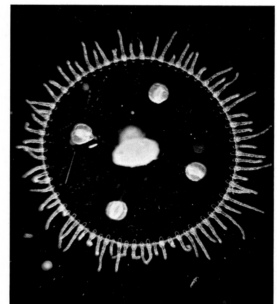

115

116

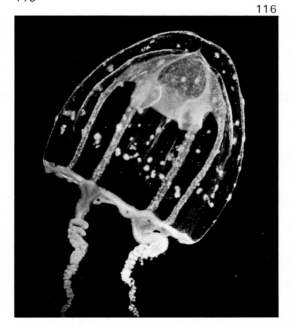

111. *Blennius* is a British crawling fish which guards and incubates its eggs above low-water mark. Besides having a scaleless skin these curious fish assist gill respiration with vascular dorsal fin web respiration.

112. The turbot, *Rhombus*, is a prized angling catch around British and European coasts and may weigh 12 to 18 kg. Mature females can lay over fourteen million pelagic eggs at one spawning.

113. Camouflaged weed fish of Australian waters crawl on pectoral fins as does the sargassum angler. As in many less active fish, parasite attack is common. An isopod clings to, and feeds from, this fish.

114. *Obelia*, though plant-like in appearance, is a rapacious predator of crustacean plankton. It can engulf copepods as large as the polyp whole. Breakdown products then circulate within the stems of the hydroid colony.

115. Calyptoblast or covered polyp hydroids have leptomedusan distributive offspring. At times plankton hauls may swarm with these pulsing, 2-mm gelatinous discs, with their four prominent gonads.

116. Some coelenterate hydroids which have naked or uncovered polyps release motile pelagic anthomedusan distributive offspring. However, since it is these medusae which have reproductive organs they are not strictly larvae.

117. Naked polyps are the distinguishing features of the gymnoblast hydroids. Usually diminutive, these plant-like animals, such as *Clava*, may cover rock faces like the pile of a threadbare carpet. Their stinging tentacles capture micro-planktonic victims.

118. *Aurelia*, the common north Atlantic jellyfish, has a phase within its alternation of generations which is a sessile hydroid. This scyphistoma, in time, strobilates to release plate-like ephyrae larvae.

117

118

In total contrast to fishes, let us now shift our attention to the opposite end of the animal kingdom. No group of marine creatures is more widely distributed than the coelenterates, a point which serves to underline the fact that success in the evolutionary game is not wholly dependent upon physical complexity. The basic coelenterate plan consists of a large sac, made up of only two cell layers, and possessing a single opening to serve as both mouth and anus. However, upon this seemingly simple plan are wrought many adaptations.

Sea jellies

The phylum is divided into three classes. The Anthozoa comprise the anemones, corals and sea pens and are all essentially sessile with a mobile larval stage. The Scyphozoa are the typical jellyfish and are predominantly free-swimming, although one group have secondarily adopted a sessile mode of life. The third class, the Hydrozoa, are the most diverse and hence the most difficult about which to generalize. Many hydrozoan species are very small and form encrusting colonies of a very plantlike form, in which particular individuals or 'persons' assume specialized tasks such as feeding, defence or reproduction. The most complex colonies and those exhibiting the greatest diversity of specialized persons are the siphonophores, members of the planktonic community of the open oceans that are discussed in more detail in Chapter 4. The life history of both the Hydrozoa and Scyphozoa is made more involved by what is usually referred to as alternation of generations – a curious cycle of sexual and asexual, and mobile and immobile phases. The scyphozoan jellyfish is generally either male or female, although hermaphrodite species are known. After the eggs have been liberated and fertilized they are often retained and brooded in the frills of the oral arms before being released as a short-lived, free-swimming planula larva. Once settled, the planula becomes a scyphistoma, a little sessile polyp, resembling the freshwater *Hydra*.

The scyphistoma is the asexual generation and,

existence, for they are born large enough to colonize littoral habitats immediately. Other blenny species guard crevice-lain eggs above low-water mark.

Another hazard that littoral fish must face is the risk of predation by birds as the tide recedes. Bullheads and sea scorpions are able to wedge themselves firmly into cracks and crevices by means of their spines, a habit that also protects them from damage when the sea is rough. Lumpsuckers behave in much the same way, but they use special adhesive organs, formed from modified pectoral fins, to adhere to the rock. In 1769 Thomas Pennant wrote of these fish: 'By means of this part it adheres with vast force to anything it pleases. As a proof of its tenacity we have known, that on flinging a fish of this species just caught, into a pail of water, it fixed itself so firmly to the bottom, that on taking the fish by the tail, the whole pail by that means was lifted, though it held some gallons, and that without removing the fish from its hold.'

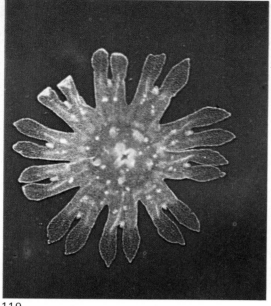

119

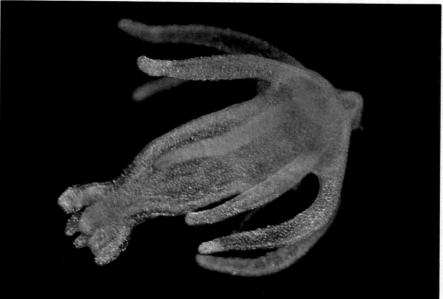

120

121

119. Distributive larvae are usually produced by relatively immobile adults. Strange then, that an active jellyfish such as *Aurelia* produces planktonic ephyrae larvae to disperse its species far and wide.

120. Few people appreciate that most shore-line animals begin their lives floating freely at the sea's surface, often miles from land. Actinula larvae are responsible for dispersing otherwise sessile hydroids like *Tubularia*.

121. Unlike most anemones, which feed by night and by day completely contract their tentacles to rest, *Anthopleura* happily feeds during the day time and has tentacles that are only slightly retractile. Some species contain symbiotic algal cells within their tissues.

by a process of strobilization, buds off a series of miniature larval jellyfish called ephyrae. The ephyrae grow into adult, sexual jellyfish and so the cycle is repeated. Ephyrae swarms are frequently encountered in plankton hauls and we have had the pleasure of filming these beautiful, diaphanous larvae in Bermuda, Australia and mid-Atlantic. To find them, however, does not necessarily mean a trip to exotic climes. Off the British coasts, *Aurelia*, the common jellyfish, produces millions of these larvae yearly.

In the Hydrozoa, there is a greater variety of life cycles. Although the majority of hydrozoans are sessile, colonial polyps in the dominant phase, some species such as *Liriope* are solely medusoid. Conversely in others, there is no medusoid stage, at least as a free-living entity. In such cases the medusae, being the sexual generation, are formed as buds on the polyps, often in a very reduced form, but not released. In some hydrozoans the planula larva is also repressed, being replaced by an actinula, a stubby, hydra-like larva that creeps about on its tentacles. A rather similar larva, the arachnactis, is found in the sea anemones. One very remarkable order of hydrozoans, the Actinulida, retains this body form throughout life, suppressing both the planula larva and the medusa. These enigmatic creatures were long overlooked and even today are something of a mystery, familiar only to a small body of specialists. They are members of what is called the interstitial fauna and inhabit the minute water-filled spaces between sand particles on beaches.

Slugs, snails and squid

In our cursory examination of the animal life of the seashore, there is one major group that we have not yet considered, namely the molluscs. Comprising the slugs, snails, oysters, squids and octopuses, the molluscs form the second largest phylum of the animal kingdom, exceeded only by the arthropods. Approximately 80,000 living molluscs have been described and a further 35,000 species are known as fossils. It is probably true to

122

123

124

say that molluscs are the most conspicuous and familiar invertebrates apart from insects. Many species are large and brightly coloured and their shells have for many years attracted the attention of collectors.

The molluscs are divided into three main classes, the gastropods, bivalves and cephalopods, along with four smaller, less important groups. The gastropods are the largest class with over 35,000 living species; it is they, not surprisingly, that show the greatest range of adaptive radiation. Nevertheless, in many respects they exhibit the least change from the ancestral molluscan body plan. A prime feature of this basic plan is the possession of a mantle cavity. This large chamber into which the excretory ducts open contains the gills in aquatic forms, but modified into lungs in terrestrial species. Ancestrally, the mantle cavity opened backwards, but in present-day gastropods, the body undergoes a process of torsion in which the entire mantle cavity and its associated structures, both internal and external, are rotated through 180° to open forwards. Torsion must not be confused with spiralling of the shell, such as one finds in snails. This is quite a different and a much simpler modification, which compacts the viscera and stabilizes the centre of gravity.

The subject of torsion is one that has fascinated zoologists for many years for it exerts such a profound effect on the whole body. All the major organ systems are displaced and the nervous system is actually twisted so that the two main longitudinal nerve trunks cross over one another. Particularly curious is the fact that some gastropods, notably the sea slugs, have secondarily reversed the process whilst leaving the nervous system distorted as evidence of their former condition. Early attempts to explain torsion were unsuccessful because they were based solely on consideration of the adult animal. Whilst there are possible advantages, such as improved flow of water over the gills and better monitoring of water quality entering the mantle cavity, there are also serious problems to be overcome. One of the worst of these is that body wastes, both from the gut and from the nephridium or kidney, are washed on to the gills. To overcome this, many species have lost one gill, so producing an asymmetrical mantle cavity through which water flows, first over the gill, and then past the excretory orifices before leaving. It is interesting to note in this context that those species in which detorsion has occurred have a reduced shell and mantle cavity and the gills are external.

The true benefits of torsion only become evident when one considers it in relation to larval life. The developing mollusc starts as a trochophore, similar to that found in annelid worms. With the enlargement of the ciliated ring or prototroch that keeps it afloat the larva becomes a veliger, one of the most beautiful and striking of all the invertebrate larval forms. Although the veliger soon starts to develop a shell, this is not fully effective protection since, without this strange event of torsion, head and ciliature cannot be fully withdrawn into the confines of the shell. Even when torsion has occurred, and the shell affords protection, all is not plain sailing, because the shell is so heavy that immediately the arms are tucked in and the opercular flap closed (if one exists) the veliger drops like a stone. This of course does serve as a speedy avoidance reaction but it can only be used in a limited way, since in deep water too great a descent could cause problems for the surface-living veliger. It might be supposed that so profound a modification as torsion would be achieved gradually over millions of years, but surprisingly this is not so. The entire process takes place within hours, during the course of larval development, and is brought about by the tensioning of asymmetrical muscles within the veliger body – a truly remarkable transformation.

Cerata and colour change

Many startling adaptations are encountered among the molluscs and one of the more striking is the defensive system of eolid sea slugs. These generally small, and often brightly coloured, shell-less gastropods are quite common in tide pools, but are generally overlooked because of their size as they creep among fronds of seaweed, browsing on coelenterates. Coelenterates possess a defensive system against predators consisting of stinging cells or nematocysts, each like a tiny harpoon with barbed head and coiled strand. In some mysterious way eolid sea slugs are able to ingest the nematocysts without discharging them, presumably by some form of temporary chemical inactivation. The sea slug then stores the nematocysts it has acquired in cigar-like projections called cerata at the back of its body. Here they provide the sea slug with protection, and the eolid advertises the fact with often brilliant colours.

Colour also plays an important role in the life of cephalopods, the most advanced group of molluscs. In most animals colour change is controlled by chemical messengers in the blood which affect the dispersal of pigments within layers of specialized cells called chromatophores. Although in its more sophisticated forms such as chameleons and plaice, subtle and complex changes may be effected, these cannot take place rapidly. Only in cephalopods does one find the ability to make

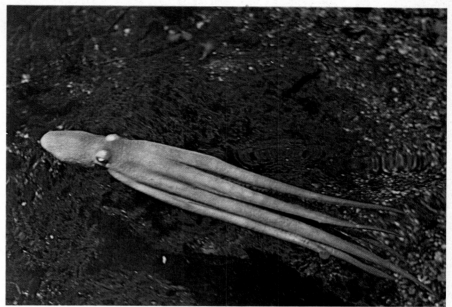

125

126

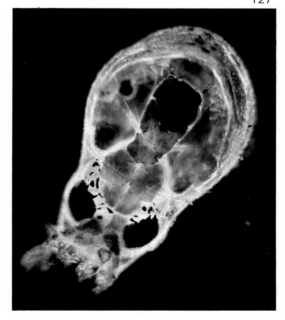

127

122. The sea slug, *Eolis*, sports cigar-shaped ceratia on its back. Eolids browse off stinging hydroids and transfer undetonated nematocysts to the ceratia for their own defence.

123. *Buccinum*, the whelk, suppresses its veliger stage by confining its larvae to life within a horny egg case. Many adult gastropods carry the shell door or operculum on the foot.

124. It is perhaps seldom appreciated that bivalve molluscs, like the scallop, *Pecten*, are able to see and swim. The design of the scallop eye is theoretically superior to the human eye.

125. Adult octopods practise rapid colour change, facilitated by muscular control of the pigment cells. Rapid flight from moray eels and rapid attack on crabs is produced by a jet-like siphon.

126. *Sepiola*, or the little Atlantic cuttle, is an actively swimming squid. It is equipped with stabilizer fins, 'hydraulic' siphon and two retractile tentaculate suckered arms, housed between the eight non-retractile arms.

127. Even the largest octopods produce pelagic planktonic larvae. Very active and predacious, these large-eyed youngsters are themselves readily preyed upon. Rapidly operated pigment cells enable them to effect speedy protective colour change.

59

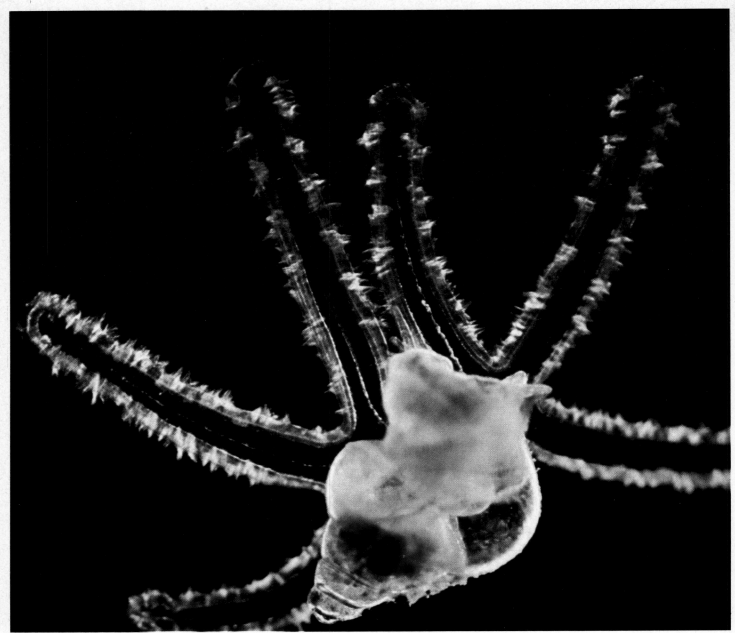

128

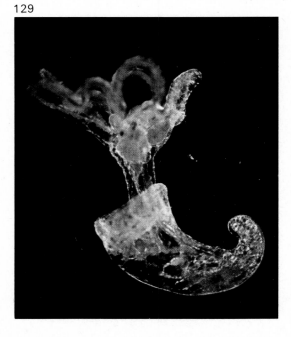

129

128. Some of the largest veliger larvae have increased their ciliated wing area to meet their vital need to swim in food-rich surface waters. If they cease to swim they drop like stones.

129. Rather like miniature transparent ammonites, there are representatives of *Echinospira* in every ocean. Both the double-keeled shell and distinct neck and head region are reminiscent of ancient cephalopods.

instantaneous changes in colour and pattern. The secret lies in the fact that cephalopod chromatophores are surrounded by a series of radiating muscle fibres which are under direct nervous control. Instead of pigment diffusing outwards to the periphery of the cell, the starlike chromatophores of cephalopods are enlarged by stretching, with no delay. The animal's colour depends on the relative size of the different-coloured chromatophores. It is an unforgettable sight to watch an alarmed octopus. Waves of colour sweep across its body as it at first tries to find a crevice in which to hide. Eventually, in desperation, it takes flight, moving rapidly by jet propulsion as it forces water out of its mantle cavity through a special siphon. As it flees it releases a cloud of ink, in which pursuers become lost whilst the octopus makes good its escape.

Throughout this chapter reference has been made at frequent intervals to the larval stages of different groups, particularly those with sessile adult forms. For many years the forces of evolu-

130

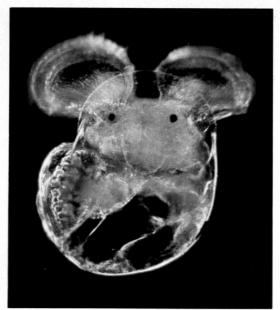

131

130, 131, 132. The larval stages of gastropod molluscs — the familiar sea snails — are known as veligers. Equipped with heavy shells from birth, they employ much energy in just keeping themselves at the surface.

133. In Australia, plankton hauls are sometimes totally dominated by veliger larvae, which swarm so energetically to the surface that they seem to bounce off it. We experienced this nowhere else in our filming career.

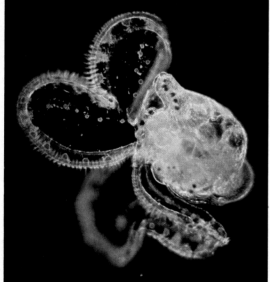

132

133

tion were considered only in relation to adult animals, these being the ones that reproduced. The possibility that there could be selective pressures acting on the larvae was not contemplated. The interest in larval forms stemmed from the belief that an animal's life history reflected its evolutionary history. Known as the biogenetic law or theory of recapitulation, this was first propounded by the great German zoologist Haeckel. Zoologists at the turn of the century therefore considered that, since many diverse groups possessed small, ciliated larvae, they were all descended from simple ancestors of this type. These in turn could be traced back to simpler jellyfish-like precursors and so on, back to the beginnings of life itself. This ill-founded belief caused endless difficulties in the interpretation of relationships between groups and the course of evolutionary history until Professor W. Garstang realized that larvae do not represent a primitive pelagic ancestral type but are a highly specialized dispersal stage in the life history.

Notochords and backbones

Clearly such larvae will all be subjected to similar pressures regardless of the group to which they belong. Small size, transparency and the frequent possession of beating cilia are, moreover, common characteristics universally shared. However, a growing larva cannot remain small, and with increasing size the problem of remaining afloat increases too. Therefore there is a tendency for the number of bands of cilia or the size of the propulsive organ to be enlarged, lengthened, or to become more and more convoluted. In mature larvae of some groups this results in ciliary bands being carried on long projecting arms stretching out from the body. Already the veligers have provided evidence of this. Perhaps the most striking and beautiful example, however, is found in the ophiopluteus larva of the brittlestars. One could be forgiven for assuming that the long arms of the brittlestar larva developed into the arms of the adult, but this is not so. In several larvae, including those of the echinoderms and nemertine worms,

134. Biologists find ascidean tadpoles — the larvae of sea squirts — particularly interesting. The larvae have vestiges of a backbone precursor — the notochord. Black dots are gravity and chemo-receptors.

135. Strange though it may seem, a mere sea squirt is more closely related to vertebrate animals than the active shore-line animals. Sea squirts have vanadium-containing blood.

the adult develops from a small rudiment of tissue, containing the gut, which at metamorphosis becomes detached from the rest of the body and settles on its own, leaving the ciliated arms to beat along, alone and stomachless, until they wither and die.

In fact Garstang's analysis of larval development in the invertebrates has led to a whole new concept in the interpretation of evolution. The old and now discredited theory of recapitulation has been turned back to front by the realization that the future evolution of a group can be affected by adaptations of the larval stages. We have already seen an example of this in the molluscs, where torsion in the larvae has profoundly affected the course of gastropod evolution and radiation. An extension of this idea, known as neotony, involves the persistence of the immature or larval body plan into adult life and maturity; for example, a tadpole becoming mature and reproducing as a tadpole without ever developing into a frog.

This interpretation of the course of evolution is of particular interest when applied to the sea squirts or ascidians. Living either as colonies or as solitary individuals, the sea squirts have an essentially sac-like form with two openings, through which water circulates, bringing in food particles and oxygen. Superficially simple as they appear, they are, in fact, highly organized animals and are placed in the phylum Chordata along with the higher, vertebrate animals. The clues to this startling relationship come from the larvae, which possess a notochord (a precursor to the backbone), a hollow dorsal nerve cord and pharyngeal slits like all other chordates. The original interpretation was that the sea squirts were degenerate creatures, secondarily sessile. However, it is now realized that on the contrary it was the retention of the mobile larval body in the ascidian tadpole, through to maturity, that in all probability gave rise to the earliest ancestral fish.

Unknowns
In this chapter we have endeavoured to give an outline sketch of the animal kingdom as encountered along the margins of the sea. In more or less random sequence most of the major animal groups have been touched upon. However, there are still a number of animals remaining that cannot be fitted into our classification; animals that may only be described as mysteries. We were fortunate to study and film the ascidian tadpoles in Jamaica in 1965. It was also there that we came upon our first unknown larvae. It is perhaps appropriate to here emphasize that even with modern advances in oceanographic research of our intertidal waters, a vast wealth of problems have yet to be solved. A considerable number of animals have yet to be found, and in the plankton community this is particularly true. Some of the unknown species we have encountered over the past few years are depicted in the three plates which appear on the page opposite. The mere discovery of new species is nothing remarkable, for approximately 10,000 new insect species are described each year. What really fires our excitement and enthusiasm is the capture of animals of

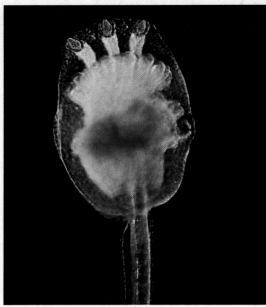

134

135

whose phylum placing we are uncertain. Future expeditions will doubtless turn up more of these mystery animals, but even more satisfying will be the discovery of clues that will help us unravel the secrets of such enigmas as our 'doughnut with tentacles', or the flaming red sphere, rotating like a great ciliated setting sun across the screen of the optical bench — an animal more in demand for inclusion in science-fiction and marine films in general than any other species we have filmed to date.

Animals: an interest for life
In looking at the bizarre and beautiful inhabitants of the seashore we have tried merely to whet the appetite for future study. The diversity of animal species, the refinement of their adaptations, anatomical, physiological and behavioural, and the complexities of their relationships and evolutionary history will provide the naturalist with intellectual pleasure and excitement for many generations to come.

136

137 138

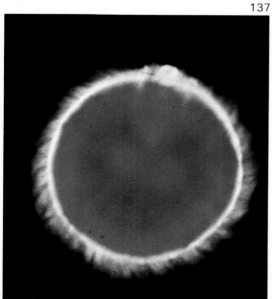

136. An unknown from the reef waters of Bermuda. This larva must be a mollusc, yet it seems to be a cross between a bivalve larva and a veliger larva of a gastropod.

137. Still unidentified, though to our certain knowledge common in Kingston Bay harbour, this 1/100-mm ciliated larva has been more in demand for inclusion in feature films than any other creature.

138. To date, this ciliated coronet has remained un-named. We found it off Jamaica, and believe it to be an actinula larva, so soft-bodied that previous surveys had missed it in formalined samples.

Chapter 4

The Ocean's Surface

Rich as the oceans of the world are in animal life, there is one area of this realm that is seldom exploited and that is the very surface of the sea. In fact, not only do most marine creatures ignore this part of the ocean, they shun it completely. Whilst it is true that in general an aquatic medium provides a more consistent environment than that which results from the more fluctuating conditions prevailing on land, the surface waters are undoubtedly the exception that proves the rule. This amazing interface may be glazed like a mill pond; or as tumultuous as Niagara. At times it is warmer than the air above, yet at other times it may be considerably colder. Through it part of the water's content transfuses into the air whilst, also through it, part of the air's content passes into the water. Whatever its form the ocean's surface is always governed by that curious phenomenon of nature called surface tension. In the case of water the surface tension is positive and therefore tends to pull itself up an immersed surface. The surface of water in a glass curls up at the edges. If the diameter of the glass is very narrow this meniscus curl can be very distinct; in a capillary tube, for example, the tension is so great in comparison to the weight of water contained that the surface tension pulls a column of water several centimetres up the tube. The surface tension of water thus helps to anchor floating objects and so prevents wind and weather uncontrollably affecting the animals that live there. Owing to the surface's proximity to the atmosphere and its constant association with the elements, winds, sun, frost, rain and snow act upon it in a way which they do not upon the vast majority of the aquatic environments. It is hardly surprising then that to live in this curious realm of sea and air demands considerable adaptive specialization on the part of the animals and plants that brave it.

We have a heritage of old sea-faring stories that tell of stranded ships afloat in seas of weed, apparently entangled for weeks at a time. Nowadays we know of the weed, but we have never seen areas of it sufficiently dense to seriously impede a sailing vessel's progress. The weed in question is called sargassum and its name has christened the area of the North Atlantic where it is believed to arise or collect. Sargassum weed looks like the common brown *Fucus* seaweed we find on rocky coasts. It is free-floating and has flotation bladders

140

139. With proboscis extended and black muscular foot enveloping another bubble of air for its raft, *Janthina* relentlessly chews mouthfuls from a capsized *Velella*, while hanging from its float.

140. There may be no message within, but several passengers stick firmly to the outside! Goose barnacles, and the occasional planeid crab, colonize bottles and sargassum weed (among other floating objects) and all drift at the mercy of wind and current.

and serrated leaves. Despite conjecture, it has never been indisputably established exactly how sargassum weed begins its existence. One theory is that a benthic sub-littoral alga growing along the coast of Florida or Brazil breaks free and, being endowed with air bladders, floats. These fragments – from 15 to 90 cm across – are able to continue vegetative reproduction, while winds and currents concentrate them into a large, slowly-circulating body of water.

Straggling slicks of this weed certainly drift north on the Gulf Stream and appear around the Caribbean and up to Bermuda. As vegetative growth continues, the size and hence the mass of each clump of weed becomes greater. The production of bladders however does not keep pace with this reproduction and they therefore impart less and less buoyancy. The sargassum weed then sinks slowly but surely. The deeper it sinks the less ultraviolet light it receives from the sun and so bit by bit the clumps die. By the time they are 100 to 450 metres down they are quite dead.

Although each clump's life may be finite and even comparatively short, there is, harboured amongst the leafy shoots of sargassum, a fair menagerie of animal life. Indeed, Caribbean beachcombers frequently come upon stranded

141. If not the most intriguing, then certainly the most grotesque member of the sargassum community is *Histrio histrio*, the walking sargassum angler fish, whose cryptic colouration has few equals.

142. What appears to be a bloom of fungus over the sargassum floats is a dense population of encrusting Bryozoa or moss animalcules. Calcareous living chambers form a lattice over the weed.

141

142

clumps of sargassum, but seldom are they aware of how much life once lived, or still does live, within the entangled mass. Adrift, hundreds or thousands of kilometres from the nearest land-fall, each clump crawls with predacious angler fish, cryptically coloured shrimps, cleverly camouflaged crabs, groves of filter-feeding moss-animals, and shoals of sargassum flying fish, to mention only a few. Yet on that sun-drenched beach amidst a dust storm of sandhoppers, the most anyone might notice would be an entangled beer bottle with a goose barnacle or two attached, and perhaps the husk of a bird-pecked sargassum crab.

Stranded sargassum weed does of course fulfil an important ecological role. Ghost crabs and migrating waders sift it for animaline morsels, while local human inhabitants collect and disperse it as natural compost. Floating, living sargassum also provides the marine community with an ecological benefit – namely a niche to exploit – for a special group of creatures that we might aptly christen the open-ocean drifters. Some depend

directly upon the sargassum; for others dependence is more indirect.

Crawling angler

It is perhaps hard to imagine a fish that crawls on 'hands' or hand-like appendages, and it may be harder still to imagine one choosing to live only a few centimetres beneath the open sea's inconsistent surface. Nonetheless, the angler fish *Histrio histrio* does both! It is an amazingly stealthy fish and displays one of the finest examples of cryptic colouration in the entire animal kingdom. Its prey-stalking is reminiscent of an African chameleon; very slow, calculatingly deliberate, hand-over-hand stalking, culminating in a sudden open-mouthed pounce. The hands are, in reality, modified pectoral and pelvic fins, the fin rays of which have become uncannily finger-like. The 'fingers' actually clasp and grip on to fronds of sargassum with an undeniable and definite clenching and releasing of the 'fist'. These somewhat human attributes immediately make *Histrio* a most attrac-

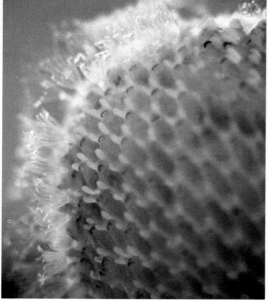

143

144

143. Bryozoan ectoprocts invaginate themselves when closed, similar to turning a glove inside out. In so doing they retreat below a miniature forest of chalky papillae and withdraw into individual compartments.

144. Fully open, feeding Bryozoa protrude fingers into the surrounding drifting waters. The powerful current produced by their countless beating cilia holds a steady residue of dinoflagellates and diatoms.

145. Every major clump of healthy sargassum weed harbours a host of permanent and casual associates. The sargassum shrimp relies on perfect camouflage to avoid detection.

146. No less well camou-flaged than the shrimps, the sargassum crabs, *Planes minutus*, frequently develop white blotches on their carapace. This may be to mimic encrusting white bryozoan colonies.

145

146

tive creature to watch and whether it be a large 15-cm female, or a diminutive 2.5-cm male, it makes no difference to its appeal. As is charac-teristic of others of their kind these anglers give a strong impression of being nearly all mouth. Vic-tims such as sargassum shrimps, smaller anglers and worm pipe-fish are dispatched in a single gulp, though presumably a good deal of 'indiges-tive rattling' goes on within the angler's stomach.

The success of this species of fish is well attested by the fact that off Bermuda, nearly every single football-sized clump of sargassum that drifts by contains at least one, and sometimes half a dozen, anglers. Their disguise is masterly and wonderful. Not only does *Histrio* look like a piece of sargassum weed – it even looks like weed complete with bryozoan ectoprocts and calcareous serpulid worm cases. Being an aquatic creature and sub-ject to the constantly changing surface currents, the *Histrio* can even move and not be noticed.

Viewed very closely with the unaided eye, sargassum weed often appears to be pilose or

147. Seen in full feeding activity *Lepas* colonies resemble animated hanging gardens of luxuriant growth. Amongst their stems scuttle well camouflaged, egg-incubating sargassum crabs, *Planes minutus*.

148. Every now and then a curious combination of oceanic associates occurs. A 2.5 cm deep-sea squid died and released its flotation shell to the surface, where a small species of goose barnacle colonized it.

149. Tar oil can act as a substrate for a host of animals other than *Lepas*. Blooms of hydroid grow so thickly that they tend to exclude other invading species.

150. Jack-sail-by-the-wind is the common and appropriate name for the 3-cm *Velella*. Millions of these attractive animals circulate around the mid-Atlantic subtropics and tropics, looking like flotillas of sailing craft.

147

furry. The 'fur' is white and surprisingly disappears every now and again. This vanishing phenomenon is soon explained by a study of the surface of the weed under a microscope. The 'pile' turns out to be a shoulder-to-shoulder colony of minute filter-feeding moss animalcules or Bryozoa. Each member of the colony lives within its own individual calcareous compartment into which it rapidly contracts when disturbed. Invariably a whole area of Bryozoa retract at once and so when this happens the pile or fur over the seaweed simply disappears. There is a second feature of the vanishing act which is rather remarkable however, and that is that in order to effect its disappearance, the little Bryozoan turns itself completely inside out. Imagine a rubber glove with fingers outstretched, for that basically is what a Bryozoan is! However, its 'fingers' are not smooth and rubbery, they are carpeted with fine, gently beating cilia which move in regular metachromal wave-like rhythm. Under high-power magnification this rhythmic beating gives the appearance of rows of

well-drilled little men marching in column, backwards and forwards. At the moment when the animal contracts it is immediately noticeable that all ciliary activity ceases, as it tucks itself into itself and withdraws quickly into its compartment. In many bryozoan species the compartment is equipped with a hinging lid – so that it closes when the animal retreats, adding the finishing touch to this micro-escapologist's act.

Also found in profusion in every clump of sargassum are wonderfully camouflaged shrimps and crabs. The shrimps have a fundamental shape that admirably resembles a sargassum leaf. In addition a wide variety of body markings adorns their bodies, providing them with realistic blemishes and encrusting growths that are typical of the sargassum leaf fronds. Like the angler fish and the crabs, these shrimps swim from clump to clump, but only when the distances involved are very short. This is because an animal so well camouflaged from aerial and aquatic predators whilst amongst brown weed can hardly expect to be equally well protected in blue-green water. What is more, the creatures concerned are poor swimmers in open water, and a badly-timed 'hop' can mean failure to reach another clump of sargassum weed, which means almost certain death.

The sargassum crab, *Planes minutus*, is similar in disguise and habit to the shrimp and more or less the same rules govern his or her life-game. However, *Planes minutus* has an additional advantage – namely that it appears to be equally at home amongst goose-barnacles hanging from driftwood, as amongst the sargassum weed. Driftwood invariably becomes smothered in goose-barnacles. It must also frequently brush past, if not become entwined in, sargassum clumps and it is presumably then that *Planes* hop from one station to another. Remarkably, it seems that amongst many 'driftwood' crabs there are usually one or two 'weedy' looking individuals. Most of the crabs, however, are exceedingly well camouflaged, with large white shell blotches and dark surrounds, so they merge well with the goose-barnacles.

Sargassum crabs and goose-barnacles

As well as their undoubted ability to be camouflaged amongst both sargassum and goose-barnacles, these little 1-cm-long crabs also show a characteristic which, as romantic humans, we may consider to be rather touching! *Planes* crabs display a marked tendency, come what may, to stick with their drifting partner. When sargassum weed rolls ashore in a summer gale, there are usually several crabs entwined within, and so left to desiccate with it on the beach. Some of the crabs must, however, make the trip to other clumps of weed, or into the open sea, before the waves throw them beachwards. This theory is supported by the fact that one seldom finds as many crabs in stranded weed as in floating weed.

The feeding habits of the crabs have been casually observed by OSF in recent years while filming them in Bermuda. While living in the weed they seem to browse on encrusting hydroids and annelid worms. Amongst goose-barnacles they nibble some of the young barnacles, but we suspect they feed mainly on encrusting growths.

Should the crabs choose to feed on young goose-barnacles alone, the supply would easily match the demand, for the rate of reproduction of the barnacles is remarkable. After six weeks the bottom of our brand-new inflatable dinghy had acquired a growth of algal filaments that looked like a deep-pile carpet, and amongst this, 2-cm-long barnacles were liberally scattered. The significance of this growth rate becomes more apparent when one observes the colony found bedecking an old scaffolding plank. Such a timber will be totally covered over its entire ventral surface and, to a large extent, over its dorsal exposed surface too. There was an initial tendency amongst those of us in OSF who had seen such dense colonies to think they were built up only over long periods of time. In reality, though, it now seems that only a couple of months at sea is enough to establish such concentrations. This of course implies that larval barnacles settle out on to the plank at a very high rate, and this is why any colony seems to be comprised of so many age groups of barnacles. The

148

149

150

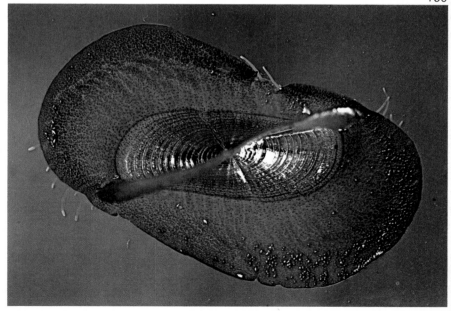

151. Awaiting a long night's exhaustive filming a congregation of open-ocean Atlantic drifters sits alongside the optical bench during our Bermuda expedition. In reality all the organisms could have drifted together naturally.

151

adult barnacles shed their naupliar larvae into the sea in enormous quantities. The microscopic larvae then inhabit the plankton community until they metamorphose into the settling stage or cyprid larva. Equipped with grappling hooks, these larvae then attach themselves to a vacant site on the plank, or sometimes settle upon an already established barnacle. A month or so later this results in what appears to be a branching barnacle! Each branch is in fact a young barnacle that settled, when it was a larva, upon the stem or shell of an already established barnacle. In this way, after a few weeks the under surface of the plank of wood becomes a waving grove of long-necked goose barnacles – each terminating in an ivory-white cluster of plates, trimmed with gold and black. Between each, glassy, sickle-shaped, sieving limbs repeatedly protrude and spread themselves into the passing, plankton-rich currents.

As is often the case with sessile marine animals, a host of other creatures exploit this living spinney for their own purposes. For example, besides the crabs already mentioned, orange polychaete worms live actually within the protective plates of the barnacle and presumably steal a certain proportion of the incoming food. Small jaerid isopod crustacea scurry between barnacle stems and glean their sustenance from settling larvae, faecal egestions and plant and animal growths.

Goose-barnacles are not only to be found on drifting scaffolding planks, nor only betwixt algal filaments on the bottom of inflatable dinghies! Showing little discrimination, they converge on almost any drifting object and on a number of static objects as well. They invariably grow on bottles, polythene containers, abandoned fishermen's floats, lengths of floating rope, boat bottoms, egg cartons, drifting coconuts, petrol cans, tin cans, blocks of expanded polystyrene, more than one species of whale, and even on lumps of crude oil! It always seems rather miraculous that anything is capable of spending its life hanging on to a small glass or polythene bottle. On the other hand, when the minute size of the grappling hooks on those front 'limbs' of the cyprid larva is considered, it becomes perhaps less surprising, for most bottles have a chip or blemish somewhere on their surface which offers an anchorage area. In addition of course, the cement glands play a major part in the anchoring process.

One of the most elegant examples of goose-barnacle colonization we saw in Bermuda was a colony of a small species of barnacle which had established itself upon the shell of a deep-sea squid called *Spirula*. It was an extremely attractive sight, but the tale that could be told around the little colony was even more appealing to us. The shell had belonged to a small, primitive deep-sea squid, rarely seen in perfect condition and which we believe has only been filmed alive by OSF. In life *Spirula* is a gleaming, silvery-white 2- to 7-cm squid which hangs in mid-deep water at a depth of a thousand or more metres. At its upper end a large light organ beams upwards while a pair of stabilizing fins flap gently to and fro. The body is shaped like a fireman's helmet – albeit somewhat elongated – and from beneath the brim stare two strange, apparently lenseless eyes, above a little clump of shrubby tentacles. Within the soft body there is a shell. Most squids have a shell, but it is usually little more than a quill. In prehistoric times, most forerunners of the squids in existence today seem to have had coiled shells, which were still largely external and so afforded protection similar to that given to snails. Some of these ancient squids had 2-metre-diameter shells and fossil hunters will be familiar with the giant ammonites from the Jurassic cliffs of Lyme Regis, for example. It is therefore not surprising that biologists today become excited when *Spirula* is found to have, completely buried in its body tissues, a coiled, chambered, partly gas-filled shell. We consider ourselves extremely fortunate too that the *Spirula* we filmed alive out in the Atlantic was externally unscarred. Usually the silvery mantle becomes abraded from rough treatment against the net mesh. In this instance, however, it was perfect in all respects, which somehow seemed to make the discovery three years later of the little barnacle-smothered shell on a Bermudan beach particularly poignant.

Oceanic pollution

We have already briefly mentioned that tar oil may be inhabited by goose-barnacles, but it is worth while giving further consideration to this – one of the worst pollutant scourges of modern times. While filming in Bermuda two years ago, we became starkly aware of the enormous amount of oil pollution in the Western Atlantic. On one beach we saw a slick of oil 4 to 5 metres long, 3 metres across and 22 cm thick. Around the slick, for a radius of several metres, all life had long since ceased. Barnacles, encrusting algae and molluscs were all quite dead. During the same filming trip we found that it was impossible to work on any beach at all without getting our feet blackened by sticky crude oil. At sea too, we were reminded, yet again, of the high level of pollution. While filming sargassum drifting 3 km off the coast, we were not aware of tar oil, but on viewing our underwater cine film when we returned, we saw

152

153

152. The bubble raft snail, *Janthina*, jabs and grabs at the mildly stinging Jack-sail-by-the-wind called *Velella*. Chance only brings these contestants together.

153. A sad end to a long journey – a 2.5 cm *Velella* lies desiccating on a Bermudan beach, in the aftermath of an onshore gale.

dozens of ugly lumps of it drifting with the weed.

In contrast to these depressing observations, however, it can be said that after a certain length of time crude tar oil definitely seems to become less toxic. This seems to be associated with its hardening and loss of the lighter petroleum fractions. It is in this state that tar oil becomes a settling surface for the planktonic larvae of some species usually found cemented to rocks. The goose-barnacle was one such example, and another we came across was an amazing 'bloom' of a white hydroid which had formed a corona over the whole lump. On yet another occasion we noticed a flatworm creeping over a small lump.

From one of the ugliest of sights at sea, crude tar oil, it is a welcome relief to turn to what must surely rank as one of the most beautiful and delicate; the little 3-cm *Velella* or 'Jack-sail-by-the-wind', as they were called by mariners a century or more ago. From a beach, pier, or inshore fishing launch it is sometimes possible to see several *Velella* at a time drifting ashore on the crest of a

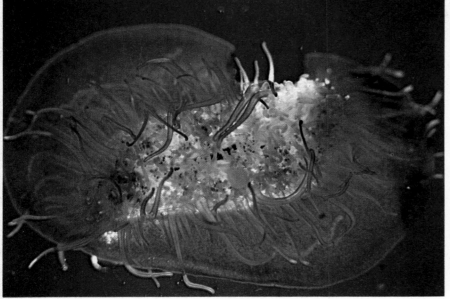

154

155

156

157

154. Floating in the surface film of the sea, *Velella* radiates a forest of small prehensile stinging tentacles into the plankton-rich waters beneath it. Paralysed victims are transferred to the central mouth.

155. The end of the line for those two mortal enemies. A rock pool harbours a *Janthina* bubble raft and two husk-like sails of *Janthina*'s usual victim *Velella*.

156. The 'up and under' technique gave us the unusual view of *Janthina*'s proboscis and radula grabbing one of the delicate feeding tentacles of a luckless *Velella*.

storm, but a storm or a good onshore blow it must be, for these little animals do not come ashore other than in unfavourable conditions. *Velella* is a true open-ocean drifter and it is one of the few that really sits on top of the surface film of the sea.

While aboard a research vessel in the North Atlantic some years ago we saw Jack-sail-by-the-winds in the sort of concentrations in which they more normally occur. To describe it as a 'flotilla' does not really express sufficiently the density of numbers involved; an 'armada' would be a more apt description – and a very large one at that! As far as the eye could see we appeared to be sur-rounded by *Velella*. Great patches of what at first appeared to be bubbles drifted by us, but nine times out of ten as soon as they came near enough for positive identification we could see they were actually *Velella*. For several hours we bucket-dipped for the 'sail-makers' and were rewarded with several perfect individuals.

It was later, in the film lab, that we really saw and appreciated the full beauty of these oceanic

wayfarers, whilst discovering, too, several things about *Velella* that we had not realized before. The diagonally-set sail has a muscular flap or vane along its border, part of which is suffused with a beautiful indigo pigment. The float beneath the sail has a glossy symmetry which reflects light like a mirror. The air (or gas) within the float produces the mirror effect, and through considerable ex-perience of filming underwater animals we have realized, in fact, how often air in water is utilized to produce this amazingly silvery effect. Around the rim of the horizontally disposed float there is a fleshy skirt – somewhat reminiscent of the rub-bery skirt of some hovercraft. In *Velella*'s case though, it is coloured anything from brilliant sea-green to deep, prussian blue or even deep purple, and it is constantly wafting and gently twitching. Beneath it radiate several tiers of azure blue, tapering tentacles, which surround a central, fleshy, blue mouth. Microplanktonic creatures, such as those discussed in the next chapter, are stung, paralysed and then killed by the stinging

158

cells if they inadvertently brush against any of these tentacles. Transfer of the victims to the central mouth is completed by the tentacles that hold the prey, bending inwards, until the mouth can wipe off the immobile captives.

Sailmakers

Seen on a calm sea, *Velella's* existence appears idyllic, but seen in rough weather this small sea-farer time and time again appears to be pounded by 'white horses'. With each pounding it turns turtle, and on every occasion it almost as rapidly rights itself. Two factors seem to contribute to this resilient buoyancy. The first is that the float and base of the sail are gas-filled, and therefore act like a rubber ball, as is demonstrated by the way *Velella* rapidly bobs to the surface if pushed under-water. The second is that the outer surface of all its exposed parts seems to be coated in a water-repellent, rather like a thin layer of wax.

Velella's sail has often intrigued biologists be-cause it is very obviously set diagonally across the

float. What is more, it has been suggested, with some evidence to support the idea, that those *Velella* found south of the equator have the sail set as a 'mirror-image' of those found to the north of the equator. The reason for this, if it be true, is perhaps that to the north and south of the equator exist two opposing currents and two opposing prevailing winds. By having sails set in opposite directions individuals tend to circulate around their own half of the mid-Atlantic.

Though tropical and subtropical in its distribu-tion, *Velella* is known to the confirmed beach-combers of UK western coasts. When it is found here though, it is usually in a very different state from that in which Caribbean beachcombers find it! In Bermuda, following an onshore gale, we found the strand line dotted with milky-blue-fringed sails, whilst on the west coast of Southern Ireland we found glassy-transparent husks, comprising no more than the float and sail of *Velella*. What then were the different factors involved in the last few hours of those two groups of *Velella*? Were the

157. For surface living organisms a vital photo-graphic shot is often 'up and under'. The optical bench enables this with the use of front surfaced mirrors and specialized lighting units.

158. Several species of bubble raft snail, or *Janthina*, occur in mid-Atlantic. Species can be distinguished by the shape and design of their raft and the colour and detail of the occupant.

159

160

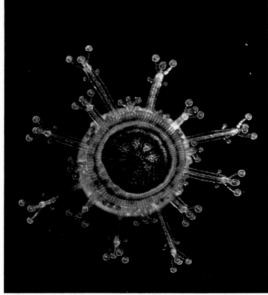

161

162

159. Seen from below, *Janthina* clings to a bubble raft laden with pink egg purses. Purses are laid one by one and each may contain 500 eggs or more.

160. Viewed from beneath, *Porpalia* radiates its tentacles. Its prehensile mouth manoeuvres to relieve tentacles of planktonic victims stung by the club-shaped clusters of nematocysts or stinging cells.

161. A dorsal float holds *Porpalia* on the surface film, while curiously clubbed branching tentacles which spasmodically flex and relax fish the micro-plankton realm beneath.

162. First seen as 1 mm black dots floating in a rock pool, these tiny creatures turned out to be one of the gems of the sea. We believe them to be very young *Porpalia*.

Irish ones simply longer stranded and therefore rotted further, or were the two circumstances rather more dramatically distinct? In reality it is probable that the Irish *Velella* had met their deaths by a much more grisly process.

In Bermuda we came upon, and witnessed in action, a strange but horribly effective *Velella*-killer. It was a snail! If a snail that lives on the surface of the sea sounds like a bit of poor science fiction, we can only say that in this case fact is indeed stranger than fiction! A beautiful lilac-coloured, purple-dye-squirting snail, up to 2.5 cm across, is definitely *Velella's* worst enemy. The snail's name is *Janthina* and is sometimes known as the bubble-raft snail.

Janthina constructs a floating raft of mucus and air and hangs upside down from it. In this manner it drifts five of the seven seas of our earth, but if it ever releases its hold upon the raft it is doomed. It would sink, and being a wayfarer of the open oceans it would be unlikely to come to rest less than 3 km below the surface. So, in a curious

upside-down manner, *Janthina* cruises around the world hanging from the surface film. Not altogether surprisingly it comes into contact with fleets of *Velella* on its journeys. As it approaches such a fleet – and this it only does by chance of wind and current – it seems to detect its future victim from a small, but finite, distance. At this point in time, this otherwise apparently lethargic mollusc explodes into activity. Its antennae curl up and out, its proboscis shoots out and its whole muscular foot flexes. The lip of the proboscis makes contact with the *Velella* and immediately takes a large mouthful out of the soft mantle. The snail's jaws or radula act in the same way as the diamond-tipped teeth of an oil-well drill, thus enabling a mouthful of tissue to be bitten off without losing grip of the victim. Mouthful after mouthful of *Velella* disappears in this way, until eventually little more than the float and the sail remain, and it is this husk-like remnant that we found in western Ireland. In the tropics and subtropics they are commonly found on beaches, and the Gulf

163

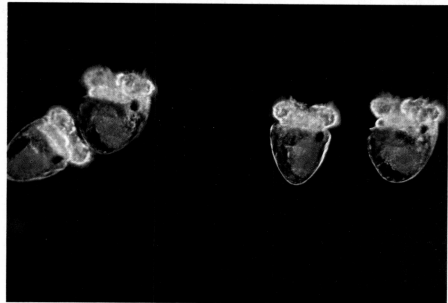

164

Stream current would have carried them to Ireland, probably from the Caribbean.

It should be mentioned that at least one other molluscan predator of *Velella* accounts for its victim in a similar manner, and that is the beautiful blue, stellate nudibranch, *Glaucus*. *Janthina* and *Glaucus* seem to be immune to *Velella's* tiny stinging tentacles. Whether very young or larval *Janthina* would be immune can only be guessed.

Bubble-blowers

The raft a *Janthina* snail makes becomes larger as the owner-occupier itself grows. It also acts as an egg perambulator. The snail deposits up to fifty or sixty egg purses on the underside of the raft. These are pink in colour and the developing veliger larvae are visible only beneath a microscope. Two or three days after being laid the egg purses show signs of life within. Ten days later they positively seethe with little larvae, each of which has a pair of rounded ciliated wings. A day or so later the purses begin to split and rupture, and out filter thousands and thousands of microscopic *Janthina*. Some of the eggs within the purses are invariably infertile and within minutes of the first successful larvae departing, the tiny predators of the plankton realm attack. These are protist ciliates which, similar to vultures, wheel in to reduce dead corpses to skeletal remains.

The newly hatched larvae enjoy a brief life of 'free flight' before their shells become too heavy and bubble rafts must be constructed to replace ciliary action by buoyancy. To 'blow' the first bubble, the larval snail must swim to the surface and with its muscular and slimy foot scoop down its first pocket of mucus-covered air.

In Bermuda in 1973, we came upon something we believe to be rather rare. In a splash pool, to one side of one of the miniature beaches on Nonsuch Island, we found six minute, blue-black, floating 'pin heads'. To the naked eye there was no detail to be seen, but on studying one under our high-power lens system, we were rewarded by one of those delightful oceanic, quite unexpected, surprises. There, filling the viewfinder screen was

what is best described as an azure-blue tiara. A central disc contained what appeared to be a glassy float. Around the float, like a spongy fender, was a heavy ultramarine coloured belt, reminiscent of the mantle we saw in *Velella*. Beneath this, twelve or more perfectly straight, radiating tentacles each ended in three or four spherical blue-green lobes. All the tentacles gently pulsed at heartbeat rate or even lower. Each of the six individuals we had found was a slightly different combination of blues, green and azure shades.

To this day we are not certain of the identity of these very small open-ocean drifters. We believed them to be relatives of *Velella*, called *Porpalia* although they would have been very young specimens. Some oceanographers have suggested that they were immature *Porpita* species. Until the full life cycles of both these species (if two species indeed exist) is fully traced and understood, it may not be possible to be precise about the identification of our rare find.

No less beautiful, yet far larger and more commonly encountered, is the notorious *Physalia* or Portuguese man-of-war. For the entire first leg of our Bermuda expedition, *Physalia* was our constant occupational hazard. We arrived on the Island of Nonsuch at about 2 pm on the afternoon of 1 April 1973. By 4 o'clock that same afternoon, we were close on 2 km out, on a mirror-calm sea, watching a pair of leaping humpback whales, while lazily trailing fingers in the plankton-rich waters around us. The latter occupation came to a rapid halt when our host, David Wingate, pointed out a full grown man-of-war not more than 2 metres from us! That was our introduction to this dangerous and strange animal – an animal that is in fact many animals. *Physalia* is like a bee swarm. It is a colony. Every member of the colony is so dependent upon every other member that the whole group acts as one animal. Each member of the colony is called a 'person'. One person is the float or pneumatophore; others are the stinging persons or tentaculozooids; others are gastric persons or gasterozooids; others are reproductive persons or gonozooids. All these strange individuals combine

163. *Janthina's* egg purses seethe with minute pelagic, ciliated veliger larvae which await the imminent rupture of their cellophane-like envelopes. As soon as the purses open, veligers leave while ciliate scavengers move in to devour infertile eggs and sickly offspring.

164. Free from their restraining parents' 'apron strings', *Janthina* veligers swarm to the surface and disperse far and wide. Soon an initial bubble of air must be gulped from the surface to form the basis of the life-sustaining bubble raft.

165. The trailing tentacles of *Physalia*, the Portuguese man-of-war, certainly extend to 15 metres, and maybe over 30 metres. It is seen here drifting through Bermudan shallows, which at a turn of wind and tide might become its journey's end.

166. *Physalia*, the Portuguese man-of-war, purposely capsizes its pneumatophore or float, every four or five minutes. This it does first to one side and then the other.

167. Well moistened, the float is slowly righted by a gradual muscular contraction along the exposed surface. This stands it on its end and a passing wave or ripple usually topples it back to its correct position.

168. Resembling a beaded curtain, the stinging tentacles or tentaculozooids of *Physalia* hang as a deadly submarine net for all who try to pass through. Individual beads are batteries of nematocysts.

169. Slung directly beneath the float and awaiting the 'food-lift' from below, reproductive, sensory and feeding persons of *Physalia* appear like an inverted shrubbery. The feeding persons expand and secrete digestive juices onto victims and consumption takes place mainly by external digestion.

165

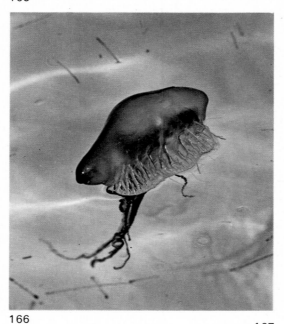

166

167

to produce one of the weirdest animals on earth – a summary of whose features is staggering. The float can be filled or topped up by a gas gland; the creature purposely capsizes its float every five minutes or so to keep its surface moist; the stinging tentacles can extend to 15 metres in length, although some reports claim they can be nearer 60 metres; the same tentacles can inflict a toxic sting capable of incapacitating a man for many days; and the gasterozooids digest the whole beast's fishy victims extracellularly.

Deadly though the man-of-war's sting may be, a small fish *Nomeus* invariably lives amongst the tentacles, thus deriving protection from the *Physalia*. These fish never appear to be stung even though they frequently brush against, and are even reputed to nibble, the tentacles. A few very specialized predators, also, seem not to heed the stings, as they eat whole, or bit by bit, living men-of-war. *Mola*, the half-tonne sun fish, is one such predator and grapsid crabs are another, although they only seem to feast on stranded Portuguese men-of-war. In the Mediterranean there is an amazing octopus called *Tremoctopus violaceus* which specializes in taking segments of still-potent stinging tentacles from *Physalia*, then holding these in its suckers so as to make use of the remaining stings to suit its own ends.

Beauty and the beast
Considering the potency of the Portuguese man-of-war's venom it is all the more surprising that a fish as attractive and apparently delicate as *Nomeus* chooses to live actually amongst the deadly beaded curtain. Beneath some men-of-war a small shoal of nomeid fish may live and while in Bermuda we saw eight fish beneath a single *Physalia*. Although we never saw evidence of these fish nibbling at the tentacles, we certainly saw them brush past unharmed. It is however worth reporting one observation that, if anything, tends to cast some doubt upon the nibbling accounts. When we scooped men-of-war, with nomeid fish, from the sea in a bucket, it rapidly became obvious that the fish were now and again receiving some degree of sting. We particularly noticed the characteristic 'wincing' movements when fish and man-of-war started to shed a lot of mucus into the water as a result of abrasion and bumps received against the side of the bucket. It was this marked and rather pathetic reaction on the part of the fish, when in a confined space with the man-of-war, that persuaded us not to attempt to film the association in the tank conditions. For this reason then, we devoted more time to filming the strange partnership in its native environment, the sea.

During the course of our man-of-war filming, the two of us engaged in the operation received stings. In both instances (one sting each), we were caught on the hand by an unseen trailing tentacle. The immediate sensation was one of intense burning and stinging. Then, despite the fact that we were probably only stung by one or two stinging cells, we both began to feel the area of maximum pain creep up our arms. Within an hour the part of the arm that hurt most was the wrist and knuckles. By the same evening the pain, which seems best described as an acute rheumatic stiff-

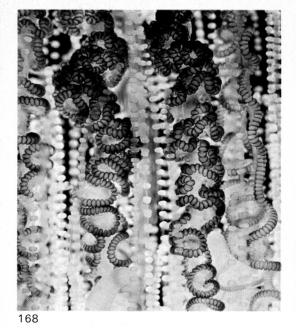

168

169

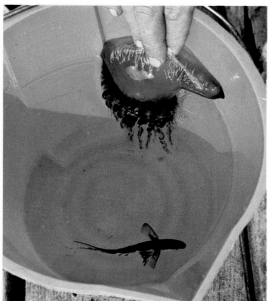

170

171

ness, had worked its way up to the elbow and shoulder. The armpit gave most pain throughout a sleepless night, and yet by morning all pain had passed and neither of us felt further discomfort. The fact that joints and armpit seemed to be affected would suggest that it is the lymph nodes that are most sensitive, once the poison has reached the blood stream.

If the way in which the sting of men-of-war manifests itself is a little diabolical, then the way in which it is actually administered is nothing short of fiendish – and could be said to be more closely associated with space-age technology than mother nature. The tentacles of *Physalia*, and incidentally those of most anemones, corals, jellyfish and Hydroids, are equipped along their entire length with rows and rows of exceedingly small explosive invertible, flexible, barbed, poisoned hypodermic syringes! These are called nematocysts and they are one of nature's incredible inventions. In the 'unfired' condition, they consist of a capsule that contains an inverted

coiled whiplash. When the nematocyst is triggered by a potential victim touching a cnidocil hair, the whiplash shoots out like a whaling harpoon – reverting itself in the process. It is shot with such force that it penetrates most animal 'skins'. The lash, being hollow and connected to a poison sac at the base, is then used exactly like a hypodermic syringe. The victim is physically restrained from struggling free by the murderous triple row of spiral barbs at the basal end of the whiplash. In just the same way as the barbs on a harpoon shot into a whale prevent the whale breaking free from the whaler, so the barbs of the man-of-war nematocysts hold its fishy victims. The poison also acts very rapidly to paralyse a fish within seconds and is said to be fatal to small children or sick people, although we have never ever heard of a fatal case on our visits to tropical coasts. Certainly however, this strange creature deserves some measure of respect for both its potency and its remarkable design and adaptation to that odd environment – the ocean's surface.

170. An inseparable association forms between *Physalia* and men-of-war fish, *Nomeus*. Sometimes a shoal of nomeids inhabits the tentacle 'zone' of a *Physalia*. Only when there is a threat of becoming stranded do nomeids forsake their hosts.

171. A stranded *Physalia* can still pack a very powerful stinging punch, yet grapsid crabs seem to relish this deadly flotsam and eat float, stomach persons and stinging tentacles alike.

Chapter 5

The Unseen World of the Upper Waters

An Atlantic roller crashes upon a jagged rock mass on the south-western tip of England. Countless relentless waves pound every Atlantic coastline – be it on the eastern seaboard of the United States or the western seaboard of the British Isles and Europe. Thousands of Pacific waves break on Indian, Australian, Japanese or South American coasts every hour or so. Every drop of water that makes up these waves and their white crests contains some trace of life. Without even being crowded each drop could, and probably does, contain hundreds or thousands of animals and plants, so small as to be virtually imperceptible to the unaided human eye. When you swallow that mouthful of salty sea next time you are bathing, think how many drops it takes to make a mouthful and when you come splashing out of the briny, dripping wet, with your hearing a bit watery, spare a thought for the numerous animals left sloshing about in your ears, or gasping in your hair! A more vivid idea of the size scale to which most of these microbes belong can be gauged by the knowledge that to catch such animals and plants, we use a net with not less than fifty meshes to the centimetre. Even so an enormous number of animals, which enter the mouth of the net, swim out between the meshes! Twenty or thirty meshes comfortably fit along the length of the eye of a needle. Look through a needle's eye then try to imagine over a hundred animals swimming through it – line abreast!

It becomes less surprising then, to hear it claimed that not only do the surface waters of all the oceans of the world contain billions and billions of life forms, but that these life forms are almost certainly the most abundant forms of life on the face of our planet. The characters with which we are now concerned are called plankton. The word means 'that which drifts' and it is descriptive of both animal and plant forms, macro- and micro-life forms, and adult and larval life stages. Larval life stages we have considered in Chapter 3 and most of the plant forms will be described in Chapter 7. It is with planktonic animals, that spend all their lives in the drifting community, that we are now concerned. Most are minute, some are just small, and a few are fair sized. All have in common one characteristic – they are at the mercy of wind and current.

173

Most planktonic animals are capable of some limited swimming movements, but these are insufficient to overcome the oceans' surface forces. Nonetheless the swimming activity of these diminutive life forms should not be ignored, since it is employed in a rather ingenious way. By means of active swimming, most of the animals we haul up in plankton nets effect what is known as vertical migration. This seemingly pointless exercise enables the animals to battle against the watery forces and to maintain a relatively constant, mean position. When you live in an ocean which directly connects two polar ice caps and several million cubic kilometres of tropical reef waters, it is rather important that you avoid being swept where you least wish to be! How then does vertical migration overcome the problem?

Most moving layers of water, especially those at or near the surface, have sandwiched between them similar layers of water, which tend to flow in the opposite direction. Thus the top four fathoms might drift east–west, the next six fathoms would drift west–east and the next three might move again east–west. The planktonic animals 'play' these layers like a Canadian log-roller uses his logs to his own advantage. By swimming vertically up into an east–wester they become transported

172. A squillid alima larva.

173. The eye of a sewing needle appears like a reinforced steel joist to the planktonic creatures in a drop of sea water. To the animals within, the drop is as large as a pond is to a pike.

174

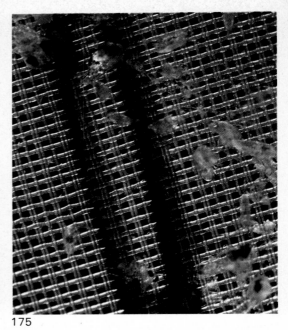

175

174. Some of the most productive surface plankton hauls are made at dusk or night. In Bermuda our night's filming depended entirely upon a thorough trawl being carried out, over the reef, at sunset.

175. The meshes of a plankton tow-net look like submarine defence cables when viewed through the 'eyes' of a planktonic organism. For most purposes nets are chosen with not less than fifty meshes to the centimetre.

176. The alima larva of the mantid shrimp is one of the larger, common planktonic organisms. This glass-like creature is so flat that it could swim through the eye of a needle if it orientated itself correctly.

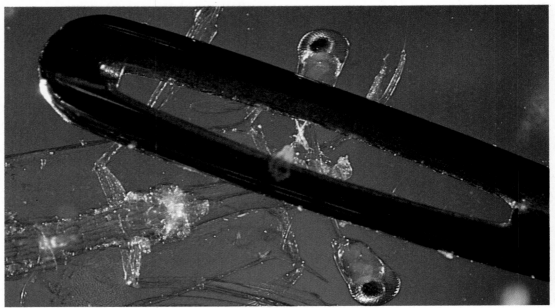

176

westwards. If, say, they do this at night, but descend to the lower layer by day, then every twenty-four hours they will have moved in a square. In this way, their mean position, over the sea floor, will be remarkably constant day by day, and week by week. So drifters these animals may be, but their powers of mobility are effective and vital to survival.

It is the vertical migration activity of planktonic animals that persuades us, on plankton filming expeditions, to trawl at night, and in Bermuda, in 1973, we found our most productive trawls came at sundown. It was then that we collected some of the more unusual mid-deep water species, which number among the most beautiful drifters of all.

Studying animals as small as these creates problems enough, but filming them can create horrendous technical difficulties. To overcome these problems, we have spent seven years evolving specialized equipment, and we have called the device a Dark Field Optical Bench. It combines mechanical, optical and lighting disciplines into an integrated whole. Whereas the prototype system

consisted of two rickety tripods clamped together at the top with two engineer's 'G' cramps, the present version consists of £7,500 worth of precision engineering mounted on its own pre-fabricated table. This same equipment has now filmed thousands of metres of plankton film; mostly for television, some for education, and some for feature film purposes.

Dark fields, dim lights

It is probably common knowledge that all natural communities have producer and consumer components. The producers are usually the plants and the consumers are those organisms which browse the plants, or feed upon those animals that browse the plants. The surface waters of the oceans are no exception to this rule of nature, and here too there are producers, such as the single-celled plants we will look at in Chapter 7, as well as consumers. One of the most characteristic features of the great, grassy plains of Africa are the vast grazing herds of herbivorous

177

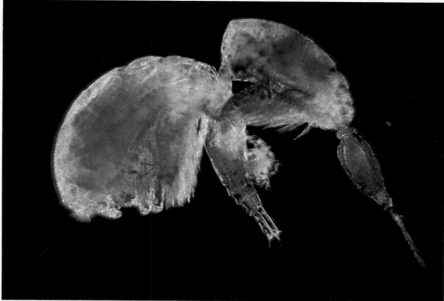

178

179

177. Some copepods lay pelagic eggs into the surrounding water, others retain laid eggs in tail-slung egg sacs. When the naupliar larvae hatch they do so all within the same few minutes.

178. For three days in succession, day-time plankton hauls were inundated with spawning and mating *Oncea* copepods. The scene in the collecting dish was a frenzy of mating activity. As many as three males sometimes tried to mate with one female.

179. Filming minute life forms presents the photographer with many problems; amongst which vibration, light without heat, and movements at right angles to the photographic axis are the most demanding. The Dark Field Optical Bench Mk. III was designed and built to overcome these problems.

antelope, wildebeest and zebra. The group of animals that fill the same niche in the oceans is the copepods.

Copepods are a group of crustacea which are probably the commonest invertebrate animals on the face of the earth. Their significance in the food webs of the sea is inestimable. The diversity within the group is enormous, and some have even turned cannibal so as to take advantage of the abundance of their own or related kind. Most are, nonetheless, filter-feeding herbivores. They have elaborate forelimbs, which waft a current of microplant-containing water through the filter-like mouthparts which in turn convey the food to their mouths. This filtering process continues much of the time enabling copepods to reap a harvest of living plant cells, mostly diatoms and dinoflagellates, which we will discuss shortly.

In the open oceans, many of the surface-living species of copepod are responsible for phosphorescence or marine bioluminescence. On two memorable occasions, this cold-fire display was afforded us and it is quite magnificent. In Bermuda, nearing the completion of a late evening plankton haul, we began pulling in the net. Time and time again at the moment of handling, the net and the collecting jar exploded into blue light which lingered a while and then waned in intensity. It is quite an eerie feeling to 'ignite' things by simply reaching out and touching them.

The second example we witnessed will always remain one of those rare, once-in-a-lifetime experiences. One night, on a research vessel in the North Atlantic the cry 'Dolphins!' came over the public address system. At 11.30 on a dark night such a call is rare so we hurried to the foredeck. As our eyes became accustomed to the dark, we could see lights appearing in the sea; momentary – but nevertheless distinct. Now and again a ball of blue fire would burn, linger and wane. Then came the real excitement. 30- to 50-metre-long trails of light streaked across our bow – the individual trails crossing with one another. These were trails of bioluminescence left by a small species of

180

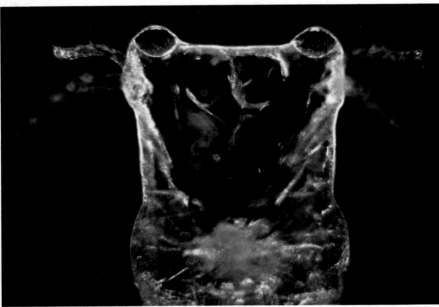

181

Delphinus, and when they neared a drifting *Pelagia noctiluca*, the big jellyfish would pulse with its own bioluminescence. Every time a wave broke, the 'white horse' would glow till the water resumed its undisturbed state. The briefer flashes of light turned out to be myctophid mid-water fish, which had, by night, migrated to the surface waters. Even the bow wave and wake of the ship was aglow. In order to check on what was responsible for the 'fiery firmament' beneath us we did a rapid plankton haul over the stern of the vessel. The net flashed at every jerk, and once on board a tap was all that was needed to trigger its mysterious glow. A single glance at the collecting can, at the cod end of the net, confirmed our suspicions – millions of bioluminescent copepods were responsible for that memorable display.

Copulative display

Anyone who has had any reason to be associated with the study of marine biology, in the field, over a prolonged period, will have experienced not only the thrill received from occurrences like the one just described, but also that given by a sudden, unpredicted surfeit of a single species. Some mariners tell of awaking one morning to find their vessel amidst hundreds and thousands of surfaced sea snakes. Cousteau recently related coming upon a mass of thousands of mating and egg-laying squid. Our experience along similar lines was a midday surface plankton haul in Bermuda, in late June. It revealed that millions of brilliant red, purple and orange copepods were swarming at the surface and mating in all directions. In many instances, two or three males were clasped on to a single female. There was really no better description than 'sex orgy'! What is more, this display of carnal desire was not a one-day affair, but appeared to go on for four days and four nights before the individuals dispersed as suddenly as they had mustered.

When a male copepod mates with a female he does not always directly fertilize her eggs, either externally or internally. Instead he may attach a cigar-shaped container full of sperm to the

182

183

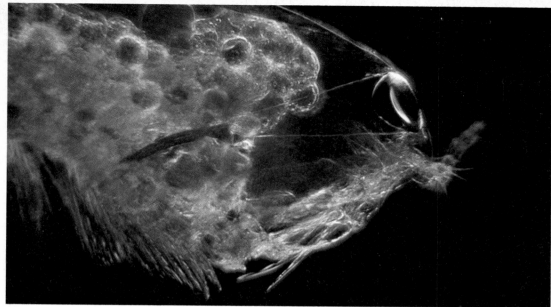

184

180. Copepods are the most numerous arthropods on the face of the earth. Not surprisingly some have evolved into carnivores; others even cannibals. This specimen continued to eat a fellow copepod while it was filmed for a television film.

181. When some species of copepod mate, the male transfers his sperm in a capsule, called a spermatophore, which he attaches to the female. She carries it until she lays the eggs.

182. Fantastic eye development is shown in the copepod *Copilia*, a species which has predated man's invention of the binocular. Enormous biconvex lenses, with external meniscus lenses applied, adorn the front of the creature.

183, 184. Seen in lateral view, *Corycaeus* displays its complex eye. Red-brown retinal material lies behind a spherical lens which presumably focuses what is relayed by the large biconvex field lens.

female. She in return 'wears' his gift and fertilizes her eggs, as they are laid, several days later.

Mention has been made of predacious copepods. There exists a fairly wide range of these marauders, and they are all well adapted to their task in life. Most are equipped with rather wickedly designed grappling or snatching limbs, and perhaps less expectedly – remarkably well adapted eyes. It is no exaggeration to say that copepods such as *Corycaeus* and *Copilia* have eye systems which closely resemble the optics of telescopes or telephoto lenses. Even more accurately they resemble binoculars and ones which probably predate man's invention of those objects by several hundred millions of years. *Copilia* is further amazing in that it appears to have employed the principle of contact lenses, or achromatic combinations of lenses, or both. It is a little difficult to understand exactly how such elaborate systems operate especially when the retinal part of the eye seems to be rather primitive. For instance, a look at the eye of *Corycaeus* reveals an enormous biconvex lens mounted into the front of the head with a very thin walled converging tube reaching back two thirds of the way down the body. This contains, near to its apex, what appears to be a spherical lens with a red pigment spot on it. Beyond this spherical lens, and still deeper within the body tissues, and nearer the apex of the cone-shaped tube, lies the rather diffused red retinal pigment.

In *Copilia* a somewhat similar arrangement exists, but with no clearly defined spherical lens near the apex of the cone tube. The most unusual feature of this complex optical system in *Copilia* is found, however, not within the animal's body tissue, but external to the large field lens where, incredibly, there is a contact lens. In the centre of the outward face of the large biconvex field lens, a thin but finite meniscus contact lens can be seen. Could *Copilia*, in the primaeval past, have evolved a system of optics only re-realized by man in the twentieth century?

Inventive though the copepods have been in their predatory designs it must be remembered that as a group they are the largest single unit within the marine community. It is not surprising, therefore, to find they are exploited by a host of other creatures. We came across a clear example of this exploitation during our Jamaica expedition in 1967. On that trip we found a large number of copepods which were apparently parasitized by a small crustacean. Later, we discovered these were the juvenile stages of cryptoniscid isopods. Sometimes, four or five were clinging to a single copepod. Little is really known about the life style of these 'hangers-on'. One theory is that they are nothing more than hitch-hikers, an example of phoresy. Another theory, which we favour, is that they are ectoparasitic and actually drain fluid material from the host copepod. This gains some support from the fact that juvenile cryptoniscids appear to have many of the characteristic features of ectoparasitic crustacea that we have studied elsewhere. Their mode of attachment seems to be too close and too tight, to be only 'strap-hanging'.

Not only is this vast animal group, the copepods, exploited by bizarre parasites or commensals, but of course they form the basic diet of hundreds of marine creatures. To quote just one example, thousands of shoaling fish snap up billions of copepods as they cruise about the oceans of the world. However, there are scores of ways in which copepods play their role within the complex food webs of marine ecology, and two that may be less frequently witnessed and yet which must account for untold millions of crustacea are when copepod meets hydroid and when copepod meets medusa.

Plant-like animals with fatal stings

Vast tracts of shore line are literally carpeted with those animals that look like plants, the hydroids. The finger-like tentacles are armed with stinging cells, and woe betide a copepod who even so little as brushes against the tentacles. Paralysis is immediate, death is rapid and ingestion soon follows. But for a copepod to be stung by a hydroid does not always mean it has ventured near the sea bed or a rock face where the sessile hydroids flourish. It is equally as possible for the

185. Even in this world of diminutives there are a host of animals which are hangers-on. It is not certain whether this cryptoniscid juvenile, clamped to the body of a copepod, is parasitic or simply a hitch-hiker.

186. Gently waving groves of hydroids bely their truly predacious nature. By simply brushing against one of those stinging tentacles, a copepod signs its own death warrant.

187. The distributive phase of many hydroids is no less dangerous to fellow plank-tonic organisms than its sessile phase, and swarms of medusae take a heavy toll of the micro-population of our seas. A copepod here hangs paralysed from a tentacle.

188. When the eggs of the onceid copepod, depicted earlier, hatch, then it is a nauplius larva which emerges. This nauplius belongs to one of the more exotic copepod species.

185

186

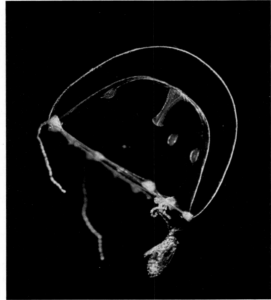

187

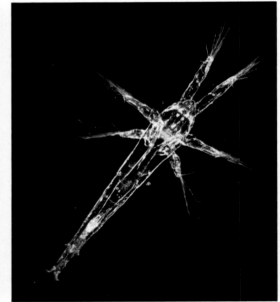

188

copepod to fall victim to a pulsating jellylike umbrella-shaped disc known as a medusa (see Chapter 3), which is the offspring of the hydroid. Equipped as they are with stinging tentacles, these little transparent soup plates are liberated by the hundreds and thousands at certain well defined periods of the year. While filming in Bermuda, we witnessed several distinct tides when the shallow warm waters around the island on which we were working became infested with hydroid medusae. A scoop with a bucket, let alone with a filtering plankton net, would capture hundreds of individuals. To our certain knowledge one medusa will take many copepods in a single day, but even such predation as this seems to affect the copepod population little. On they swarm, on they filter and on they breed to liberate more naupliar larvae, some of which will survive to restock the adult copepod populations.

One of the most compelling factors in encouraging anyone to observe and study planktonic organisms is that one never knows what a haul will contain. As with fishing, there is a peculiar fascination about dipping beneath that relatively impenetrable interface and hauling out something very alien to our terrestrial existence. Sometimes the capture is a big thrill, sometimes a big disappointment and sometimes – surprising though it sounds – it is a big laugh!

Comedians

Some of the marine plankton are just natural clowns and no group is better at clowning than the molluscs, especially the pteropod and hetero-pod species. These delightful animals swim so peculiarly and are so strangely modified to suit their odd existence that the sight of them always inspires wry humour. However, these beautiful molluscs will be discussed in greater detail in the next chapter, so suffice it here to say that North Atlantic waters abound in several species of limacinid pteropod. 'Pteropod' refers to the wing-like foot, the violent flapping of which produces a clumsy but directional flight path.

189

189. Pteropods are wing-footed molluscs which occur in enormous numbers in both inshore and open ocean waters. The wing surface is ciliated and wafts a layer of mucus towards the mouth which entraps micro-organisms on the way.

190. It was in the surface waters of Bermuda that we actually witnessed *Phronima* devouring a live salp from the inside out. We shall discuss this animal in greater detail in the next chapter.

190

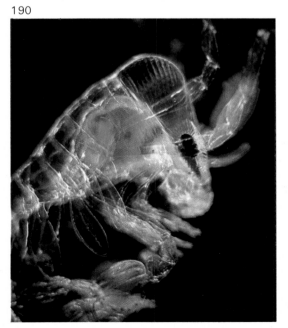

The heteropod molluscs have always struck us as being amongst the very strangest of marine microplankton organisms. Sculling as they do with their single median ventral wing they prescribe an unusual rolling, twisting course, yet they do not lack a fair turn of speed. The heteropods we encountered in Bermuda belonged to two genera, namely, *Atlanta* and *Carinaria*. Since the second species occurs in mid-deep waters, we will discuss here the shelled species, *Atlanta*, with its large shell, elephant-like trunk, and cylindrical eyes. The eye is doubly distinct since it has a distinctive black stripe which passes straight through it. This sort of eye stripe is usually considered to make the tell-tale eye of its owner less easily noticed. However, it is hard to believe that such a stripe has any effect upon those animals that might attack *Atlanta* or might instead be about to fall victim to it, so we can really only guess at its role here. *Atlanta*'s trunk is a proboscis and within it, a serrated, abrasive radula or tongue is held in readiness to tear layers of flesh from whatever

191. Limacinid pteropods proved to be a common constituent of the reef plankton community in Bermuda. This genus retains the coiled snail-like shell of regular gastropods.

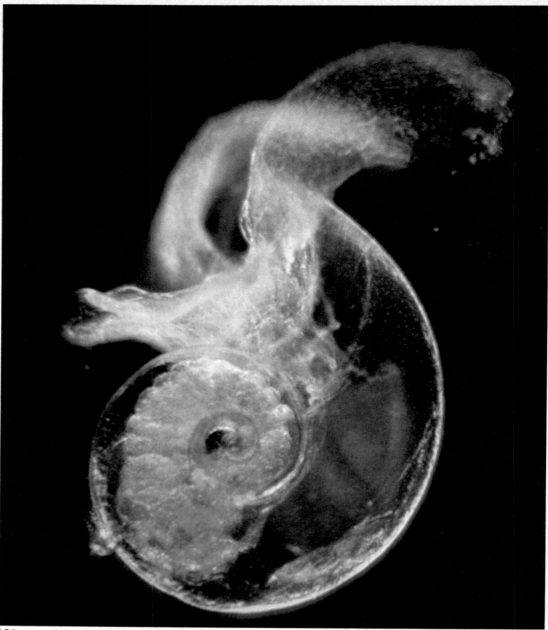

191

luckless planktonic creature falls victim to it.

The rich ochre and brown colouration of *Atlanta* is in marked contrast to the ice-like transparency of the two groups of planktonic animals we next consider.

The first group would in some ways have been better described in Chapter 4 where one of its close cousins was described. Like a cluster of synchronized booster rockets *Agalma* is a pulsing, throbbing relative of the notorious Portuguese man-of-war. In Bermuda, one overcast morning, when onshore winds swept flotsam all around our landing stage, we dipped a small hand net into the middle of a scum of dredged-up turtle grass filaments. Amongst these strands of weed we found thousands of small medusoids and amidst them one beautiful, perfect siphonophore, called *Agalma*. We then realized that a 'pink ribbon' found in the bottom of the previous day's trawl was in fact the central rachis of this species. In good condition, the central stalk of this animal subtends two dozen or more swimming bells,

topped by a flotation pneumatophore (this is the big float in the Portuguese man-of-war).

Below the swimming section of *Agalma* is a region of reproductive individuals, and below these are housed the highly contractile fishing threads which are bedecked with stinging cells. These threads can extend 30 cm or more, and must certainly secure a steady supply of hapless planktonic creatures from the surrounding waters. Like the man-of-war, *Agalma* is a colony of individuals, not just a single individual. Every individual depends upon every other individual, and no 'person' can survive alone.

Salps and squirts

Several of our sundown hauls in Bermuda supplied us with a host of small transparent barrel-shaped animals. These were the 1cm long, very beautiful pelagic salps; a group of animals similar to sea squirts that have abandoned their hitherto sessile existence during which they were clamped on to rock or pier pile. When first viewed, in a col-

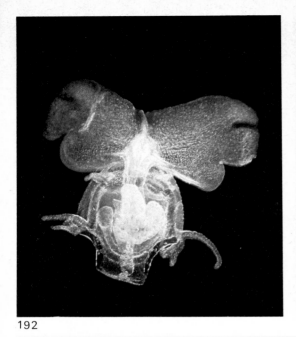

192

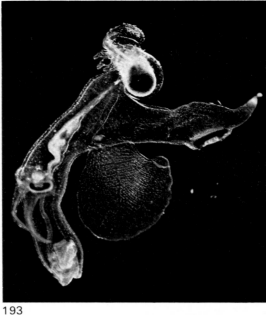

193

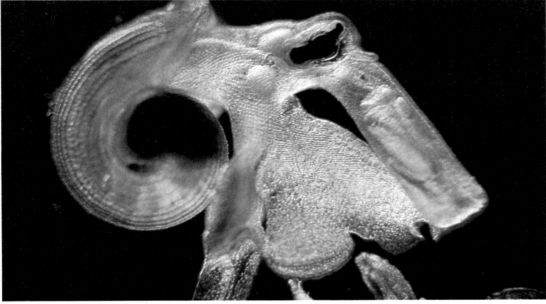

194

192. The cavoliniid ptero-pods have evolved a bivalve-like shell. Short hind spurs are parts from which shrubby body extensions can be protruded. These may reduce the rate of sinking when the animal ceases to 'fly'.

193. Although this larval carinariid heteropod was only 0.5 cm long, its adult counterpart, in the dimly lit depths of the open sea, may attain a length of 30 cm and can deliver a painful bite.

194. The heteropod molluscs include, in their ranks, some of the weirdest animals on earth. *Atlanta*, one of the shelled species, is a predacious animal which feeds upon any animal it can catch — especially other molluscs.

lecting dish, the animals themselves are seldom spotted. What is much more obvious is the jostling and bumping which is characteristic of salps.

Salps, in the open Atlantic, may grow to a fair size; for example a salp called *Ctethis* is fully 10–15 cm in length. However, even the smaller species, with individuals only 1 cm long, can appear much longer when first viewed. This is because some salps practise a degree of colonialism, forming into chain colonies, which may extend for some 50 cm. On a research vessel in the Atlantic, fairly recently, a group of biologists awaited a bottom sledge-trawl and its contents. When it came aboard everyone made a beeline for the cod-end and its contents. Far more exciting and beautiful to my way of thinking was the delicate 25-cm-long chain of salps strung like a stiff glass necklace over the head rail of the trawl. The sight of such a colony is fairly common to an oceanographer, but it provided me with three happy hours of filming and photographing. With their 'jet-engine' type of propulsion, these de-

lightful animals are more reminiscent of the space age than of the primaeval past from whence they came.

It was through filming close relatives of salps, namely their sessile cousins the sea squirts, that we first became aware of the truly amazing heart system possessed by most of the tunicates, as they are called. Some years ago we mounted a biological filming expedition to Jamaica. It was during the marine work of that trip, more exactly during our work in the mangrove swamps and lagoons, that we first observed sea squirts closely. In close-up, we filmed the very spectacular open transport blood flow and, in turn, the heart that pumps it, and were intrigued to find that the heart operated in a fashion we have never encountered in any animal other than a tunicate. The principle of the heart is as nearly that of an archimedean screw, for lifting water, as mother nature can manage. The impression is that a spiral membrane beats within a closed tube. Perhaps even more strangely — the direction of beat, and therefore

195. Little more than a floating mouth, 8-cm-long *Beröe* comb jellies, or ctenophores, hover around drifting swarms of sea gooseberries and lobate ctenophores upon which they primarily feed.

196. The apparently harmless sea gooseberry, *Pleurobrachia*, is equipped with two retractile tentacles, armed with sticky lasso threads. Like a balloon trailing its tether, it drifts through surface waters rich with planktonic fish larvae, upon which it feeds.

197. Juvenile *Beröe* comb jellies move very rapidly when compared to the adults. The implication is that the size of the comb plates changes little with body growth, so with a small body progression is rapid.

198. Pelagic sea squirts or salps, like 3-cm *Salpa*, have mastered the art of propelling themselves with a reciprocating water jet. A series of muscle bands pulses rhythmically to expel a repetitious jet of water.

of blood flow, reverses once every 75 beats or so. Could this be to back-flush the 'backwaters' of the open transport network? If this appears to be side-tracking slightly, it does also relate to the pelagic as well as the sessile tunicates. *Salpa* is the pelagic species most commonly encountered in the North Atlantic.

One final claim to fame for the tunicates is the obscure fact that their blood contains a rather unusual element. Whereas our blood contains iron in the form of haemoglobin, the blood of sea squirts contains vanadium, no satisfactory reason for which has as yet been proposed.

As equally transparent as the pelagic sea squirts or salps are the sea gooseberries, which are a delightful group of animals. Strictly speaking, this fisherman's term is applied only to an animal known to biologists as *Pleurobrachia*. However, *Pleurobrachia* has a number of cousins, all of which are loosely referred to as sea gooseberries. As might be expected, the name arises from the animal's resemblance to the better known fruit, and the feature which is most 'gooseberry-like' is in fact common to all the relatives.

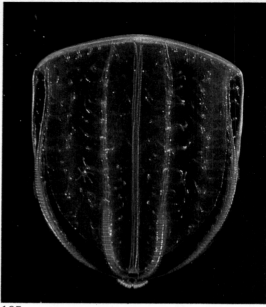

195

Comb jellies and cerceria
Sea gooseberries are sometimes found stranded on the beach, and in this unhappy state pass for rather uninteresting blobs of firm, transparent jelly. Seen, however, in mid-water with the light coming predominantly from beyond the subject, the 'blob' becomes quite magical. The main body pulses with light reflected from the eight rows of comb-plates or fused cilia. Each plate is highly refractive and in certain lights can give a beautiful display of interference colours, with every spectral colour represented. From the central spherical mass may extend two long fishing lines up to fifty times the length of the body, and with a hundred or more side branches. These side shoots all seem to be equispaced from one another and each is parallel to its neighbour. The whole spectacle thus becomes one of amazing symmetry and delicacy, and yet, one is strangely aware of a merciless predator awaiting its victim. Shoaling, as they often do, an area of sea may be swarming with sea gooseberries and such a fleet of animals may account for countless millions of commercial fish larvae. Such predation is well documented in North Sea fishing tales. The fish larvae are captured on the sticky lasso threads which carpet the tentacles of *Pleurobrachia*. Stuck to the threads the victims are wound to the mouth by the sea gooseberries spinning on their own axes.

It would be wrong to think that all ctenophores look, or behave, like *Pleurobrachia*. Some, for instance, have no tentacles. The incredibly delicate lobate ctenophores, like *Mnemiopsis*, look like the most diaphanous silk as they hang in mid-water. In Jamaica, we used to come upon mixed swarms of *Pleurobrachia* and *Mnemiopsis*. Regular as clockwork, every morning, as the on-shore day breeze replaced the offshore night breeze, making the water in Kingston Bay as calm as a millpond, the sea's surface off the end of Port Royal pier was dimpled and puckered with the bodies of ctenophores and a species of medusa called *Liriope*. When we scrutinized these early-

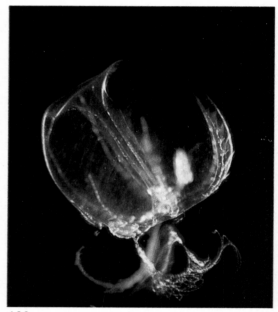

196

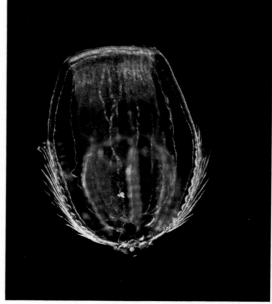

197

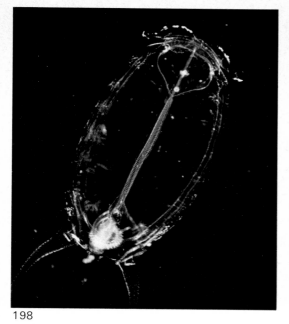

198

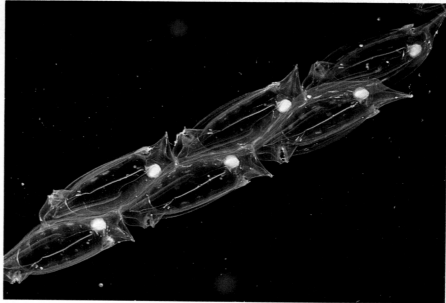

199

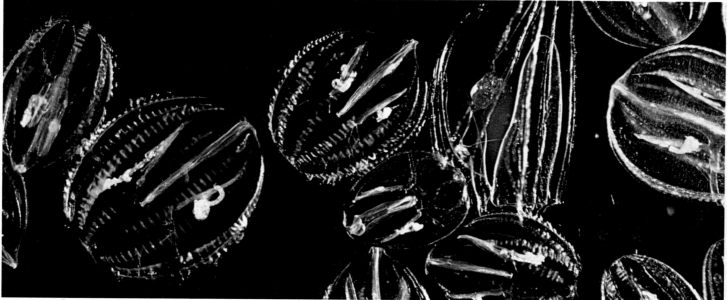

200

morning swarms, we always found the two species hitherto mentioned, but in addition, there were invariably large numbers of *Beröe*. *Beröe* is a 5–8-cm ctenophore which feeds specifically upon other ctenophores, and in a spectacular way at that.

Beröe is best described as an animated swimming mouth. It paddles up to sea gooseberries and lobate ctenophores and opening wide its large lips, it clamps on to the outside of its cousin. The victim ctenophore rapidly turns from transparent to opaque in the area of the lips. A colleague and I once witnessed such an attack, but the odd thing about it was that the predatory *Beröe* was one-sixth the size of its victim. Nonetheless the little killer rapidly converted the lobate ctenophore into a crippled, opaque mass.

We have mentioned earlier that swarms of planktonic animals may lead to a plankton haul being dominated by a single species. Some of the hauls we made in Bermuda were dominated by fish eggs. Many fish lay pelagic or floating eggs;

pilchards do for example and their eggs are cigar-shaped. Pelagic eggs drift and mature at the surface, ultimately to hatch as minute fish embryos carrying yolk sacs, which provide their first few days' food supply.

To buoy up both eggs and hatchling embryos each individual is endowed with a flotation device. In most fish a small oil droplet is all that is usually required. The droplet appears as a perfectly spherical object inside the perimeter of the egg – a globe within a globe.

Although, when they attain a certain size it would be incorrect to term juvenile fish 'members of the plankton', nonetheless as young and old alike they do, in a way, give rise to a host of planktonic larvae. These larvae are parasites of fish and are invariably passed out of the gut with waste products of metabolism. When they enter the sea, they are in a very motile stage of their life and in a plankton sample they are usually recognized by their frantic activity. In Australia recently, we found plankton samples often contained

199. Some colonial salps are 2 or 3 metres long, but *Iasis* seldom measures more than 30 cm. Complicated life cycles, vestiges of backbones and vanadium-containing blood make salps biological mysteries.

200. Vast swarms of glassy-transparent pleurobrachiid and beroeid comb jellies, and the occasional siphonophore, dimpled the surface of the mirror-calm waters of Kingston Bay harbour in Jamaica almost every morning of our three-month stay.

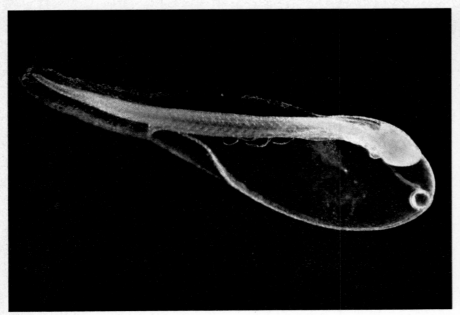

201

202

201. Fish emerge from their eggs as yolk-laden larvae which remain in the plankton community for several weeks. Feeding mainly upon copepods, they themselves fall victim in their millions to comb jellies, medusae, siphonophores and arrow worms.

202. Parasitic flukes have complicated life cycles with several larval and/or distributive phases. The phase of the cycle which attacks the primary host is the motile cercaria, a 2-mm tadpole larva.

203. The primary hosts of most marine flukes are fish, and the extreme motility of all cercaria suggests they have to make a concerted dash for their fishy dwelling place when an opportunity presents itself.

204. The alima larva of the squillid or mantid lobster is one of the commonest and strangest large planktonic larvae. They are found in plankton hauls over the continental shelves.

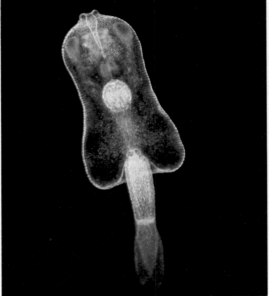

203

204

bright yellow cerceria larvae of fish liver flukes. These larvae are the stage that parasitize the fish. In turn, they have arisen from a parasitic stage in a mollusc or copepod, which is known as the redia stage. The secondary host was, in turn, infected by a free-swimming miracidium stage.

Filming in the tropics on one occasion, I witnessed a fluke (not a liver fluke) departing from its copepod host. The life cycle of this particular fluke was unknown to me and it was difficult to guess at its next destination in the open sea. The fluke was nearly half the size of the copepod, and its departure was grotesquely reminiscent of a tape worm leaving a dog after treatment for the parasite – not a pretty sight.

Worms and flukes, such as we have discussed here, are all termed endoparasites, because they live inside their hosts. The converse of endo- is ecto- and an example of an ectoparasite found in the plankton community of the ocean surface waters is a type of louse called *Caligus*. *Caligus* is actually a modified copepod. It is frequently found

firmly attached to its host's body – especially near the base of pelvic or pectoral fins, where it secures a meal of its host's body fluids and flesh. *Caligus* is not infrequently found as a free-swimming animal; presumably on its way from one fishy host to another, and it is then that it can be picked up in plankton trawls. In many ways, *Caligus* has paralleled the evolution of *Argulus*, the freshwater fish louse. The curious thing is that the two animal groups are quite distinct and only very distantly related.

Larvae from below

In this chapter so far, we have mainly discussed those unseen animals that spend all of their lives in the upper waters of the oceans. We have, on the whole, left the coverage of those animals that live as larvae in the upper waters and as adults on the ocean floor to the chapter concerned with the unseen world of the seashore. However, before leaving the realm of the photic zone – that is the well-lit surface water where micro plants abound

205

− we must make some reference to those animals which, though bottom-dwellers as adults, do not really come into the seashore context. Yet they liberate millions of eggs and larvae into the plankton-rich surface waters, thus distributing their kind far and wide.

It is reported that much of the floor of the French and English Channel is carpeted with millions of brittlestars. Every one of these liberates eggs which hatch into tiny planktonic larvae. This example is admittedly a spectacular one, but many thousands of others could be described in which the adult animals browse, burrow, grub, slither and slide over the ocean bottom, while sending aloft tiny planktonic distributive larvae. From amongst the thousands we have chosen just one interesting one to describe here − that is the larval stage of a bottom-living lobster which operates rather like a praying mantis.

The lobster is a squillid or mantid lobster, and it shuffles around the warmer sea floors of the world, taking refuge beneath rocks. Some species are

large and good to eat. All are capable of striking a rather formidable blow at enemy and prey alike. The mantis-like front limbs are also found in the larva, which is sometimes called the alima or phyllosoma. The latter term refers to the very flat and transparent nature of the larval squillid. It is one of the largest larval forms encountered in the tropical and subtropical plankton, and it was for me the first memorable impression of a four-month plankton filming expedition to Jamaica. What impressed me, particularly, was that only the pale yellow tips to its backwardly pointing carapace-spines showed up, as it swam erratically around the collecting dish. It has ridiculously large eyes on the ends of long stalks and the blocks of muscle inside its mantid-like forelimbs, when seen with dark-field illumination, produce a spectacular blue interference colour.

So, all in all, the photic zone of the oceans boasts a very mixed batch of unseen animals, all of which are directly or indirectly dependent upon the real microbes of the sea (see Chapter 7).

205. The stalked, compound eyes of this crustacean appear as two isolated black dots in the collecting dish. So transparent are the body and limbs of the 1-cm squillid larva, that it is often noticed only hours after the haul is first examined.

Chapter 6

Life in the Ocean Deeps

No other biological realm on this planet remains so little known, so little explored and so little researched as the ocean depths, which range from 100 metres to eight or nine kilometres. What research and exploration is done in this field is carried out by oceanographers from chemical, physical, geological and biological disciplines. All the research is highly specialized and the equipment and methods used are sophisticated. However, there are a number of general principles which if explained and understood from the outset will endow with a sense of appreciation and respect all those of us who are lucky enough to work with the researchers and their assistants. Here, only the biological aspects can be commented upon, but each discipline must presumably have its own peculiar problems.

With deep-sea biological research, we are dealing with the most three-dimensional sampling domain in the world. On land we tend to think in terms of two dimensions – left and right, and fore and aft. Up and down is, by comparison, seldom explored. Animals do not dig far into the ground and only a very special few exploit the air above about fifteen metres. In the deep oceans, however, it is very different. We may be dealing with three to eleven kilometres depth of water, and all of it inhabitable water – that is, the element that covers by far the largest area of the earth's surface.

Water covers seventy-one per cent of the globe. In conjunction with the incredible vastness of this domain, we should also not forget that our sampling method, to tell us what lives within this realm, is so 'pint-sized', it is almost laughable. On land, aerial surveys, capture-release techniques, netting methods and visual counts are all employed to give scientists fairly accurate assessments of population numbers, species and migrations. All these techniques are largely impossible with creatures that inhabit the ocean deeps. The following fairly vivid illustration of this remarkably low sampling percentage is worth mentioning.

One of the bulkiest deep ocean-sampling techniques involves a net, which is the size of a large sitting-room, being towed for many hours at depth. The procedure is as follows. The closed net and its acoustic-control gear is lowered overboard from a research vessel which steams at two knots. 7,000 metres of cable are payed out over a one hour period. When all 7,000 metres of cable are

out, the net may be 4,000 metres below the surface. At this juncture a signal is relayed to the control gear which opens the mouth of the net. The net is then towed, open, for four or even six hours. It is then closed and hauled. The tonnage of water filtered by that net must be astronomical, and yet fewer creatures than would fill a washing-up bowl arrive at the surface. In spite of this (apparent) extreme paucity of catchable life, some of those creatures in the washing-up bowl are amongst the commonest life forms on the face of this earth. Some must be numbered in their billions. All this, then, is another way of saying that the oceans comprise an incredibly gargantuan biological realm.

No light, no plants
This realm – the realm of the deeps – has a number of other strange features worthy of mention. For instance, if you chose to live in the midwater deeps, you would have to get used to knowing no interface other than the bodies of other creatures. You would never see the surface, and only in death would you ever touch the bottom – if then. The depth at which you would live is too deep for seaweeds to exist. The nearest thing to an interface that you might experience would probably be the thermocline, that rather enigmatic, quite well-defined boundary between relatively warm water above and cold water below. In general terms, the upper layer circulates slowly, and so picks up warmth from the surface waters. The lower layer is amazingly static and constant in all respects. The animals that live in the depths, for the most part, experience little or no light. Some of the deep-water species migrate to the surface at night, some never come near the surface. Correspondingly, some have extremely enlarged eyes, others only vestigial eyes.

However, it would be incorrect to imply that all those species which remain in the lightless depths have vestigial eyes or retarded sight – many have neither. Hence it is pertinent to query the reason for eyes and sight, at depth. Like so many of the observations made on deep-water species, no simple answer to this exists. It does, however, seem certain that some of the ocular development seen in mid- and deep-water animals is associated with perceiving bioluminescence, that strange ability of some animals to

206. Not infrequently, 30-cm periphyllid jellyfish enter trawl nets down to 1,000 metres depth. Usually dead at the surface, the specimen seen here defied death, reattained neutral buoyancy and stayed thoroughly alive for hours!

207

208

207. *Cavolinia* pteropods flap clumsily through upper Atlantic waters. Sargassum-like drogues trail from 'ears' at the shells' hind edge.

208. Remarkably similar in design to its surface-living cousin, the deep water *Limacinid* is sepia brown and relatively large — 2 cm across its shell.

209. Mid-deep-water pteropods include species like *Clio* in which the transparent shell has become streamlined.

210. *Clione* is a predacious midwater pteropod which occurs in considerable numbers. Shoals of these quaint shell-less molluscs flit in search of their shelled cousins through the dimly-lit depths.

211. 5 cm long and so transparent that they are truly invisible in a white dish, *Cymbulia* is a curious pteropod which has developed a boat-like neo-shell hood.

212. *Pterotrachea* is a 10-cm heteropod which has dispensed with a shell and which sculls itself with a single median fin.

213. The cranchid squids utilize ammonia as a buoyancy agent within their body cavity.

214. *Gonatus* frequents depths in excess of 200 metres, where it actively hunts small crustacea. It was this animal which gave us a most spectacular display of pigment cell activity.

209

210

211

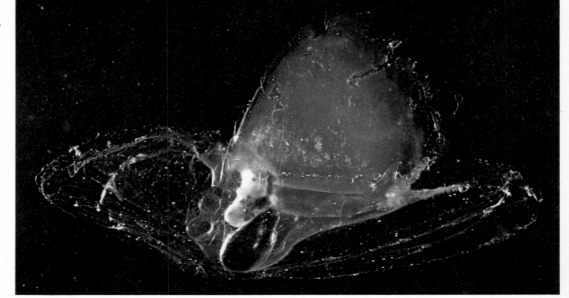

give out a cold light, produced by chemical processes within their own bodies. Whether this light
is used in defence, decoy, courtship, alarm or
intraspecific signalling is not known. What is
known is that the organs producing this peculiar
light are so elaborate, diverse and organized that
we are forced to the conclusion that their
presence is of great significance to their owners.
Who would have believed, for instance, that one
of science's more noteworthy achievements of
the last thirty years would prove to have been
pre-empted a few million years ago by a deep-
water fish?

Precedents in nature
There is almost a cult, nowadays, for proving
that nature thought of nearly everything first
– parachutes/dandelion seeds, helicopters/syca-
more seeds, tough elastic fibres/spider's silk, the
gimlet/certain wood-boring wasps and their ovi-
positors, and so on. These examples are simple,
but of quite a different category would be fibre-
light guides; those remarkable bundles of glass
fibre, with the flexibility of polythene, which will
conduct light introduced at one end straight
through to the other, whatever bends may occur
along the length of the bundle. There lives a fish
in the mid-deep waters of the Atlantic which has
been known to science for many years. Its name
is *Opisthoproctus*. Only a few years ago, a research biologist had a close look at the curiously-
placed anal light organ of this very flat-bottomed
fish. When he cut open the ventral surface of the
fish, the biologist was amazed to find two relatively enormous fibre-optic bundles leading from
the light organ across the entire ventral floor. It
seems probable that in this way, the light arising
from the anal light organ is conducted all around
the ventral periphery of the fish. It is hard enough
to explain how such a system could possibly have
evolved, let alone to hazard a complete explanation of how such a device could now operate.

A second example of extreme or elaborate
adaptation also hard to explain is that afforded by
a large group of mid-deep water squids. Histio-
teuthid squids, and squids from several related
genera, have very large eyes in relation to their
body, but the really amazing feature is that the
right eye is four or five times the size of the left eye
and in structure, totally different. Both eyes,
furthermore, are ringed by a number of specialized
light organs, but the arrangement round one eye
is very different from that around the other. It has
been suggested that one eye is used at depth,
while the other is modified to operate optimally
at shallow depths, when the squid migrates near
to the surface. However, some recent analysis of
the lens and retinal characteristics of the two eyes
indicates that this is unlikely to be the case.

Strange physical adaptations
So there we have two examples from dozens of
extreme adaptations of deep-water animals to
their environment; two examples, which are both
inexplicable, and as such typical of so much to do
with the unseen world of the ocean deeps. It is to
be hoped that those who are patient enough to
read this chapter will not judge too harshly the

212

213

214

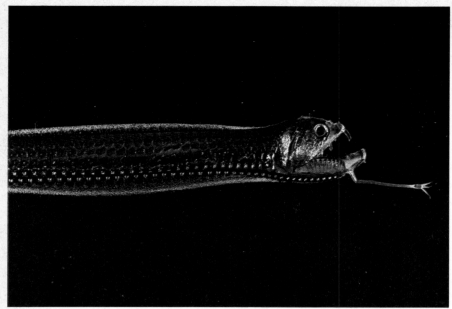

215

216

217

inadequacy of the explanations offered for some of the truly incredible physical adaptations.

To the strict evolutionary or taxonomic biologist, the order in which these phenomena are described will seem odd. However, since this chapter is not intended to provide a comprehensive coverage of mid- and deep-water oceanic life, there seems little merit in pursuing a discipline pertinent only to the specialist at the possible expense of the general reader's interest.

Some snails and some slugs, in contrast to the proverbial pigs, have wings, and, in underwater terms, might be said to 'fly'. Most of us probably think of the ocean deeps harbouring weird and wonderful creatures. Not wanting to shatter this illusion, it seemed only right to begin with a group of animals which can surely claim to be some of the oddest on earth. The enormous phylum Mollusca contains two particularly strange groups; the heteropods and the pteropods. Pteropod means wing-footed and *Cavolinia* is a wing-footed snail. It is also an open-ocean animal that lives fairly near the surface, and so acts as an introduction to this unique but plentiful realm of life.

'Flying' snails

Cavolinia is a robust, 2-cm-long creature which invariably arrives at the surface, via the trawl net, retracted. The smooth, beige shell is all there is to be seen. The first time we came upon one in the catch, experience with shelled molluscs had taught us years before not to be deceived by initial appearances, so our retracted *Cavolinia* was placed in a bowl of fresh sea-water along with more active ingredients of the catch. Two hours later in the darkness of our research-vessel filming lab, we were so intent on filming some other animal that a loud tinging noise failed at first to attract our attention. Suddenly, we realized the *Cavolinia* had sprung to life and was performing a memorable dance around the bowl in which it was placed. The thought of that heavyweight pteropod 'tingalinging' around inside the metal dish, crazily flapping its ridiculous wings, still makes us laugh, and its flapping continued in mid-air while it was being transferred to a filming tank.

Since that time, the delightful cavorting of pteropods of several species has provided us with many attractive film sequences. Pteropods, however, have a number of elegant features about them, and all are interesting. The open-ocean *Cavolinia* provided us with such a feature. From the two short spurs at the trailing edge of the shell, our *Cavolinia* slowly sprouted sargassum-like extensions. Research colleagues told us that seldom before had this been seen. The purpose of the extensions is not easily explained in an animal not otherwise associated with any weed formations. It does, however, seem that it can only be some type of floating weed that this pteropod attempts to resemble, both in its overall colour and its weed-like extensions. *Cavolinia* inhabits the upper 100 metres of the Atlantic. In death, however, its shell carpets acres of the ocean floor.

Three other species of pteropod enter nets trawled in the North Atlantic. Two are very dark, and one is as transparent as glass. *Clio*, one of the dark species, has curiously slate-purple wings and

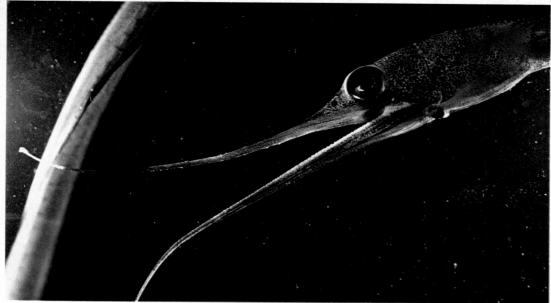

218

215. Of all ocean denizens, fish are the quickest to capture the laymen's interest. *Stomias* is found at depths of 700 metres and seldom exceeds 35 cm, unless, that is, larger ones escape the trawl net!

216. Characteristics of a stomiatoid fish are a chin lure which bioluminesces, widely gaping wicked jaws, large eyes and rows of regular light organs. The hunting habits of the fish we can only guess at.

217. *Chauliodus* has a jaw mechanism and design not unlike that of an inverted sabre-toothed tiger! Small wonder then that it appears to be one of the most capable, swift predators of the ocean depths.

218. The snipe-eel *Nemicthys* attains a length of 75 cm, and has been seen to hang motionless, and vertically, in the twilight zone while lying in wait for sergestid prawns.

a shell like a pair of lightly tinted polarized sunglasses; transparent enough to see through, but effective in reducing the glare! It seems odd that at a similar depth there occurs a pteropod called Venus' slipper or *Cymbulia*, with wings, body, and attractively ornamented shell as clear as crystal. The shell of *Cymbulia*, in a white dish, simply cannot be seen. Only with fierce back-lighting is there a chance of seeing this structure in detail. The effort of setting up this sort of illumination repays the effort, for the shell is designed like a spacecraft-cum-speedboat, and strangely seems to be a neo-shell developed from a different part of the body from that of most pteropod shells. Longitudinal ridges sport regularly-spaced rows of glass hooks. The front end is keenly sharpened and flared, like a cross between a heavy artillery shell and a Citroen car. A posterior port seems to permit feeding access of the soft body-contents to the outside world. It is said that this boat is in fact a hood and that the wings protrude ventrally. Cine footage of *Cymbulia* does not substantiate this theory. *Cymbulia* seems to occur in considerable numbers in some parts of the Atlantic, since every now and then a mid-water trawl comes to the surface containing dozens of specimens.

Deep-water camouflage
The second dark-coloured species of pteropod encountered in these North Atlantic trawls was a species of *Limacina*. Surface-living, inshore limacinids are common around European and American coasts, and most are like perfectly ordinary land snails, but in the marine version, a pair of flapping extensions replaces the slowly creeping foot of terrestrial species. The deep-water *Limacina* is charcoal black except for its shell, which is a rich dark tan colour. One of the curious features about many limacinid pteropods is their swimming activity. Whereas when a bird flies through the air the wings beat up and down while the body remains still, when a limacinid pteropod swims the wing stroke is so pronounced that there is a tendency for the body to be affected by it. At times one even gets the impression that the wings are

still and the body is going up and down. In the depths at which this deep-water species is found, namely 1,000 metres or so, there can be little or no visible light available. That light which does exist is unlikely to be sufficient to show up this 'study in black and sepia' and this species of *Limacina* must be as invisible as a black cat in a coal-hole.

Not all pteropods possess well-defined external shells. *Clione*, or what we affectionately call the 'flying angel', is such a pteropod. It is very soft-bodied, yet retains its characteristic shape. Judging by the number sometimes caught in trawl nets, large shoals of *Clione* may ply the mid-waters of the North Atlantic. Their typical pteropod wings flap clumsily, and when in full flight their progress can only be described as humorous. I have never met anyone who does not laugh when shown film of *Clione* at 'lift-off', yet *Clione*, for all its quaintness, is a rapacious predator of shelled pteropods.

A joke of creation
Snails without shells are usually thought of as slugs; those that live in the sea are understandably called sea slugs. There is however a group of snail relatives, with little or no shell, which are distinct from nudibranch (naked gill) sea slugs, and these are the weird and awesome heteropods. Looking at one of these outlandish animals, be it a 30-cm *Carinaria* or a 2-cm *Pterotrachea*, one cannot help thinking that God, at the time of the creation, somewhat tired of rhyme and reason and streamline design and decided to have a little fun creating heteropods. Consider this: heteropods have shells so small they only house the heart and gills; tongues exactly like wood rasps; eyes with tubular retinas and plano-convex lenses which seem in no way able to focus light on to this retina; a drogue parachute flap used for goodness knows what; a trunk like an elephant; and a median ventral fin, used exactly like the single skulling oar from the stern of a boat. Furthermore, it is said that a large specimen of *Carinaria* is capable of delivering a painful bite.

Some years ago we were asked to contribute

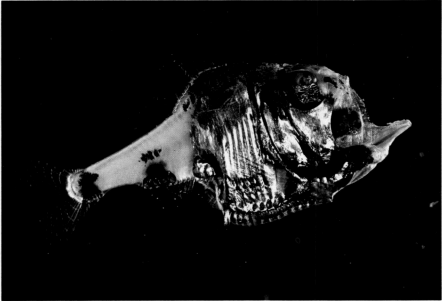

219

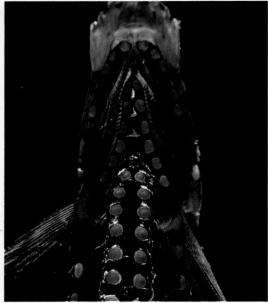

220

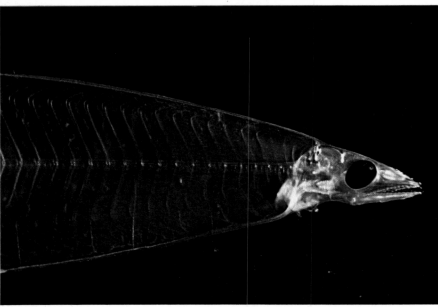

221

222

some footage to a feature film, footage of sea creatures of the very weirdest type – something no one was likely to have seen, and something no one would be likely to forget! We suggested that close-up filming of some of the more unusual planktonic creatures from the sea might fit the bill. Accordingly, several thousand pounds worth of expensive 35-mm cine filming equipment was shipped to a small island off the coast of Bermuda where we had set up a film studio for just such work – but for television purposes. Some of the ghoulish animals we chose for inclusion were these ridiculous heteropods, and one of the species was the surface-living larval stage of *Carinaria*.

In a separate group of the molluscs, yet quite closely related to pteropods and heteropods, are the cephalopods or squids. Mid- and deep-oceanic waters are inhabited by some truly amazing squids and octopuses. The creature with one eye four times the size of the other has already been mentioned: the mid- and deep-water squids are no less strange.

Eyes, beaks and suckers

Squids and octopuses, in general, represent the most advanced evolutionary achievements among molluscs. Amongst the squids we have one of the largest invertebrates on this earth, namely the giant squid *Architeuthis*. These enormous cephalopods are known from two sources; the scars on the skin and the beaks in the stomachs of deep-diving sperm whales, and strandings on various shores. Adult giant squids can with no exaggeration range in size from 5 to 10 metres long.

Size is not the only, or by any means the most noteworthy achievement of cephalopods. The development and function of the eyes of squids, and indeed that of the whole nervous system, is in some respects as advanced as our own. Molluscan eyes, and certainly those of squids, are designed in such a way that their owners do not look through their own, albeit transparent, optic nerves. Man, however, does look through his own nerve branches, supplying the retina. Squids have an

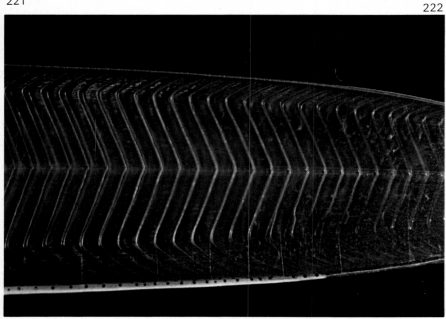

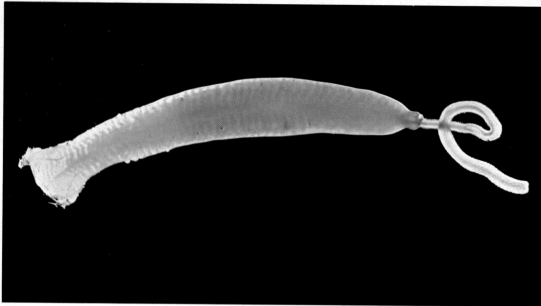

223

extremely advanced and flexible propulsion system with different gears and two entirely separate modes of progression. Surface-living squids display a marked degree of social behaviour and there is no reason to believe that some of the mid- and deep-water species do not exhibit similar tendencies.

A deep-water squid called *Pyroteuthis* has eyes that, in relation to the size of the rest of the body, are probably the largest in the entire animal kingdom. The generally well-developed eyes of squids seem also to go hand in hand with their ability to bioluminesce, or give off their own cold light. 'Galaxies' of light organs seem to cover some squids and in the case of *Pyroteuthis* some of the light organs even reside inside the body cavity, but since many squids have translucent or transparent tissues, little is lost to the viewer.

Most squids seem to be able to regulate their buoyancy. In this way relatively effortless hovering in mid-water can be achieved. The large group of mid-deep-water squids, known as cranchid squids, have evolved a buoyancy system that would appear to pre-adapt their owners to life on one of the less clement planets, for this group of molluscs maintains its buoyancy by means of an ammonia-filled gland, the contents of which are presumably regulated by the owner. Many cranchids are also transparent and so too are all their organs except the liver, which is highly silvered and therefore reflective.

Man's general dislike of octopuses and squids possibly stems from such fictional works as Jules Verne's *20,000 Leagues Under the Sea*, in which a loathsome, monstrous squid attacks a submarine craft. The spectacle of groping arms, with suckers like soup plates, is all that is required to send shivers down most people's spines. However, marine biologists and the Easter Islanders know that suckers and arms are not the real danger of octopus and squid attack. Far worse is the eagle-like beak situated within the fleshy folds of molluscan mantle. This beak in the case of the giant squid is a football-sized piece of biological engineering with a muscle system almost as

powerful as a hydraulic press. These enormous beaks are only known from the stomachs of the squid arch-enemy the sperm whale. But perhaps still larger squids inhabit the deep oceans. No whale, no trawl technique and no submersible craft exists that can supply us with evidence for or against the existence of such giants. Nevertheless it is an intriguing and not unreasonable thought that such leviathans could exist.

If visions of deep-sea squid create nightmarish effects upon some people, then so too do the similarly distorted fantasies relating to deep-sea fish. Line drawings in books have contributed considerably to these speculative hallucinations. Granted, the facial characteristics are enough to alarm anyone, but what few people realize is that the subject of their nightmares is only the size of a child's fist. Let us not underrate the amazing and bizarre adaptations of deep-sea fish however, for amongst these vertebrates we come upon some of the world's most wonderful and, in the biblical sense, awful creations.

Large mouths, larger meals

Any fish with a name like *Stomias boa* is likely to have rather strange looks, or habits, or both. The stomiatoids are a group of carnivorous fish which, in common with many deep-sea animals, are equipped with mouths capable of making short work of most of their fellow creatures including those of their own size. Some of the deep-sea carnivorous fish have arrived at the surface with fish more than their own size, either in their stomachs, or sticking out of their mouths. Records of such finds seem to have immediately entered the annals of fishy tales and as in many of those stories, there is sometimes an element of exaggeration. Like so many aspects of deep-sea biology, we can never be too sure of our facts. Maybe those gargantuan meals were genuinely in the process of completion when the trawl-net swiftly scooped the contestants from the depths, but many biologists believe that the meal started in the trawl-net, and that only the abnormal juxtaposition of those animals, in that situation, forced

219. When trawled, argyropelecid hatchet fish seldom reach the surface alive, since swim bladders distend with reduced pressure. Upturned eyes and gape imply copepod and cyprid prey is grabbed from beneath.

220. Could ventrally placed and downward directed light organs, which in life glow with a pale blue-green light, imitate overhead twilight? Biologists believe 7.5-cm *Argyropelecus* disguises its presence in this way.

221. Tales of the European freshwater eel and its spawning migration to the Sargasso Sea are legendary. The hatching eels develop into leptocephali, so called because of their leaf-like appearance.

222. Under normal lighting conditions, leptocephali are totally invisible in water except for the black eye. With intense dark-field illumination, muscle somites radiate beautiful interference colours.

223. Unsegmented 5-cm pelagonemertean worms are found only in the deepest waters, several thousand metres down. Their relatives live in tropical rain forests and rock pools.

224. One of the commonest mid-deep water jellyfish is the beautiful 7.5-cm-diameter *Atolla* which normally lives at depths ranging from 500 to 1,000 metres.

225. One is fooled into believing that these beautiful colours function at depth. An unnamed jellyfish makes us puzzle yet again over the use of colour in the ocean depths.

226. Freshwater cyprids are less than a millimetre long. 2.5 cm giants with parabolic reflector eyes live down to 1,500 metres and are aptly called *Gigantocypris*.

the meal ever to commence. If an animal is equipped with a mouth that opens to an angle of more than 120 degrees and its jaws are fringed with teeth like those of a sabre-tooth tiger, it should come as no surprise to find it has bitten into its nearest fellow-victim in the trawl-net. Be that as it may, many of these carnivorous fish do have incredible feeding-habits. A great many sport lures from either chin or snout. *Stomias boa* has a handsome chin lure with a large light organ at the tip. No one is absolutely certain how these lures are employed to entice would-be victims, but by comparison with the angler fish of less deep waters which are invariably equipped with either or both types of lure, it is fairly certain that the lure is waggled, or flicked, or trembled, or lit up so as to attract the prey. A satisfactory enticement is then bound to be followed by a swift lunge with mouth agape. Such captures must be quite spectacular in the murky depths since both captor and captive are almost certain to emit light at times during the event.

The stomiatoids are very well endowed with light organs, and apart from the prominent facial ones, the whole of the body is covered in a layer of bioluminescent jelly which surrounds a pile of curious clubbed spines. How this body covering and its associated bioluminescence are employed by their owner can only be speculated and, probably, anyone's guess is as good as anyone else's.

Abyssal sabre-tooth

One of the most frequently encountered deep-water 'tigers' is *Chauliodus*, which has a mouth exactly like a sabre-tooth. The gape of the mouth is enormous and is mostly produced by the dropping of the lower jaw to a ridiculous extent. Nonetheless, the whole skull seems also to tilt up on the end of the spinal column, so lifting the upper jaw at the same time. *Chauliodus* is an example of a deep-water creature which for all we know might attain 6 to 30 metres in length. As far as authentic records go, it barely exceeds 60 centimetres in length, but consider for a moment yet another problem of deep-ocean sampling. Most deep-water trawls open with a mouth which might be 5 metres across and 2 or 3 metres deep. This net is trawled through the murky depths at a speed of less than two knots. At that speed almost any animals of size would, with little effort, take evasive action and avoid the jaws of the net. It is quite possible that most of the larger fish detect the oncoming net minutes before it is upon them. So it may be many years before oceanographers can tell us definitely whether or not really large creatures inhabit the ocean's depths. Direct observation may, furthermore, be the only way of determining the truth.

It was by direct observation, from deep-diving submersible craft, that the habits of the extraordinary snipe eel, *Nemicthys*, were discovered. As its name suggests, this fish has a bird-like beak, but unlike those of most birds the jaws of the snipe eel widely diverge at their tips. For many years biologists wondered how the rasp-like inner surface of these divergent jaws could conceivably operate. The technique of food capture, as seen by scientists from the diving craft, consisted of this fish

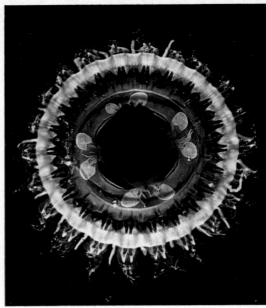

224

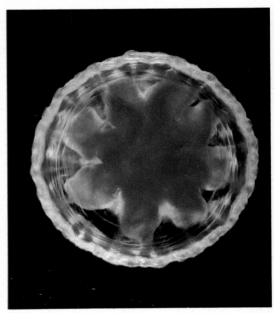

225

226

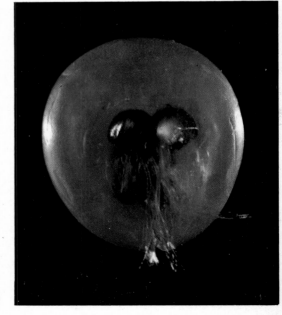

227

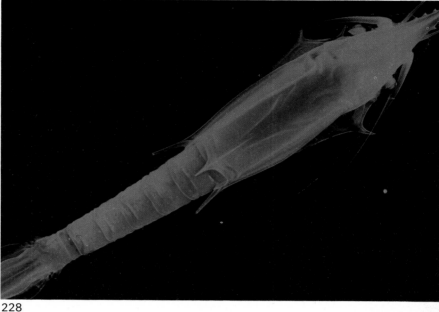
228

229

227. Surface copepods are mostly small and transparent, but those like *Bathycalanus* and *Megacalanus* from 1,000 metres are crimson, maroon or orange. They measure up to 5 cm across the antennae.

228. For a group that are seldom more than 2.5 cm long, this 10-cm scarlet mysid called *Gnathophausia* is enormous. Found down to 2,000 metres it is believed to filter-feed or scavenge.

229. It is hard to believe that at 1,000 metres a 12.5-cm scarlet *Ephyrina* appears as black as pitch. Even luminescent secretions could never produce wavelengths capable of showing this colour.

'standing' vertically on its tail. That, for any fish, is strange, but for a fish one hundred times longer than it is deep, it is extraordinary. With head up, and jaws agape, the fish were seen to hang in midwater and in this attitude, were seen to latch on to the enormous antennae of vertically migrating, descending, sergestid prawns. So we see that strange behaviour is linked with strange adaptations. The mind boggles, therefore, at the possible behaviour that is linked with some of the other more extreme physical adaptations seen in other deep-sea creatures.

Sometimes, deep-sea nets come to the surface clearly having engulfed part of a shoal of fish. The hatchet fish, or argyropelecids, are believed to shoal in moderate numbers. These are one of the fish most noticeably affected by the transference from deep waters to shallow. Seldom, if ever, do they reach the surface other than eviscerated, their swim bladders distended so much that they – or other body contents – protrude grotesquely from the mouth. It goes without saying that but

for the odd shudder or twitch, hatchet fish are dead on reaching the lab. on board a research vessel. A great many people think that all deep-sea animals reach the surface in this state, but it should be understood that in reality only fish with swim bladders suffer in this way. Some fish suffer far less, and all animals without air bladders are more likely to suffer the affects of temperature increase, net abrasion, or excessive illumination than they are from anything relating to pressure change.

On first sight in the hand or the net, hatchet fish look remarkable. Besides being incredibly reflective, they are extremely flattened from side to side, they have turret-like eyes which gaze forever upwards, and if turned ventral side up, they display a regular battery of pink-coloured light organs. It is the production of blue-green light from these organs that is often the final vestige of life on the part of the fish. With the aid of an image intensifier and a well-versed research biologist, Peter Herring of the Institute of Oceanographic Studies, we suc-

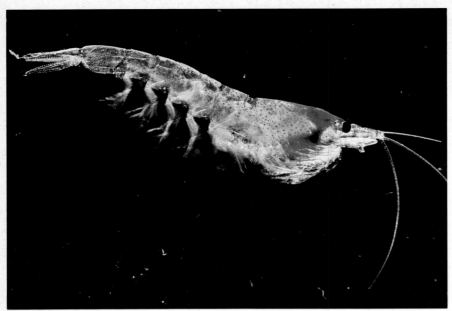

230

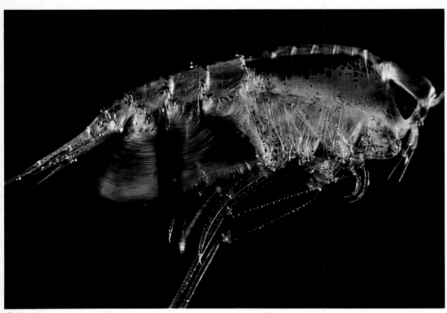

231

232

ceeded in 1973 in filming this spectacular bio-luminescence, and it was possible to demonstrate vividly how directional the light was. All the light organs beam their light vertically downwards. It is said that, seen against the mid-water twilight filtering from above, this eerie light renders the fish well camouflaged from predators below. The silvery sides perform a similar function for laterally-approaching predators, and when seen from above the dark countershading on top of hatchet fish makes them indistinguishable in the murkiness of the deeps.

The functional significance of those heaven-directed eyes is not understood. One species of hatchet fish feeds particularly upon giant ostra-cods. However we do not know how these fish approach their intended victims. Is it from below, gulping with J.C.B.-like jaws, as the animated cherries swirl above them?

Glassy larval eel

If hatchet fish are designed to avoid detection by devices like mirrors and light organs, then the unbelievable leptocephalus larvae of eels achieve the same end by glass-like transparency. An 18 cm leptocephalus eel larva, swimming around in a white dish on the deck of a research vessel in the North Atlantic, is invisible – totally invisible – but for its black eyes. So all one sees is a pair of closely-spaced black dots. The crystal-clear body, seen under intense back-lighting, is a beautiful spectacle. It is comprised of V-shaped muscle blocks, called somites, and each of these displays a gorgeous sheen of interference colours. This causes the whole animal to resemble a pale silk scarf, which catches the light as it turns and twists. The muscle blocks are otherwise quite transparent – one could even read a newspaper through them! The diminutive spear-shaped head displays, through its glossy skull, filamentous gills and teeth, and a curious gill-like filament inside the nares. The story of the reproduction of the European freshwater eel is too well known to describe in detail, but suffice it to say here that most of the strangest stories about them are true. They do migrate over land on their way to the open sea and the ocean depths beneath the Sargasso Sea. They do migrate to the Sargasso Sea at depth – along the ocean floor, and they are seldom caught in nets en route. Their breeding behaviour is almost totally unknown. What distinguishes, in development, the American eel race and the European eel race is also far from understood. The exact sensory physiology of the larval eels returning to fresh water maybe 10,000 or 11,000 kilometres from their birthplace is largely still a mystery. The miraculous metamorphosis from leptocephalus larva to river-estuary elver is often seen and studied, but not too well explained in terms of adaptive function.

It is an intriguing fact that many salt and fresh-water eel adults have leptocephalus larvae. When full-grown, these larvae range from one-eighth to one-sixteenth the length of the full-grown adults. Imagine then, 18-cm larvae becoming 180-cm adults – and worse, imagine the horror of a biologist presented with an almost 2-metre-long larva. It is said that perhaps this true fact is the

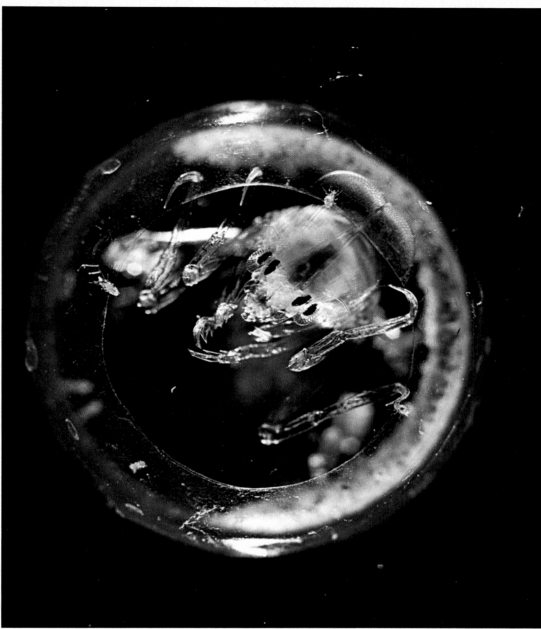

230. Euphausiid shrimps abound in all oceans. Many have developed powerful ventral light organs. Dense shoals migrate to the surface at night and cold water species include whale 'krill'.

231. Of all the crustacean groups, amphipods seem to have conquered ocean depths the most successfully. *Parathemisto*, which lives at several hundred metres depth, eats rosacean siphonophores from the inside out.

232. Some of the deep water amphipods retain tough resilient exoskeletons. Usually, the deeper living the species, the softer its external tissues. Fragile species like the one seen here hail from below 2,000 metres.

233. A female *Phronima*, in her self-shaped *Pyrosoma* barrel, views her twilight world with four compound eyes. Two of them keep constant watch on the realm above.

234. *Phronima* partly devours colonial salps, and then uses the remaining test as a perambulator for its saddle-shaped cluster of offspring. The parent propels the house and aerates the youngsters at the same time.

233

234

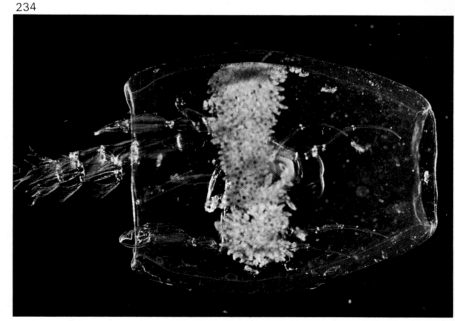

strongest evidence for an authentic sea-serpent.

If we now return to the invertebrate members of the deep-sea community we enter a realm of beautifully coloured life forms. Yet these colours are destined never to be seen as we may see them. Some are destined never to be seen at all. For an object to appear correctly coloured it has to be illuminated, and moreover, to be illuminated by white light. Therefore, if a red object is illuminated with blue light it may appear dark brown or even black. The brilliant mid-yellow nemertean worm, with proboscis extended, might appear a dark, ghoulish green when observed in the dimly-lit depths. Nemerteans, or unsegmented worms, are a strange enough group, as demonstrated by the 12-metre-long bootlace worm on a rocky British shore or the brightly-striped species which abound in the leaf litter of tropical rain forests. When they add the ocean deeps to their environmental conquests, their weirdness is doubled.

It may seem odd to many people that deep-sea animals are often very brilliantly coloured. Though

235. Brachiopods were more commonly found on earth 400,000,000 years ago, but they still remain today in one or two special niches. *Lingula* is a benthic species found at 2,000 metres.

235

why should they not be? We do not so readily question why the intestines and vital organs of humans are brightly coloured. For a characteristic to survive in the evolutionary progression of all life, be it colour or structure or behaviour, it need not necessarily, once it has appeared, confer advantage on its owner. It must however not confer disadvantage; not, anyway, until after reproduction has been successfully achieved. Conceivably then, some deep-sea animal colours are a byproduct of metabolism or physiology that does not lessen the survival chances of the individuals concerned.

The deep-sea jellyfish are among some of the most beautiful denizens of this strange realm. One of these, frequently brought to the surface in mid- and deep-water trawls, once gave us a rare half hour on deck. The species was that bullet-shaped jellyfish *Periphylla*, a beautiful beast, but invariably lifeless in the bottom of the net. On this particular occasion, a good-sized specimen, about 15 cm overall, was caught and was seen to be pulsing strongly. Placed within the filming tank, this diaphanous animal displayed its unusual ability to assume neutral buoyancy. It proceeded to hang in mid-tank, touching nothing. This it would do for two minutes at a time and then it would rapidly flap its way surfacewards. These jellyfish are believed to make lantern fish and crustacea their staple diet.

Another deep-sea jellyfish is *Atolla*, and like *Periphylla* it is coloured with this unusual mixture of maroon and white, but *Atolla* also has a beige pattern within its disc. To me, both these species of jellyfish are indescribably beautiful. Their colours and textures are most sophisticated and subtle.

Parabolic 'headlamps'
Earlier in this account of some of the deep-sea fish it was mentioned that one species of hatchet fish feeds upon *Gigantocypris*. To say that *Gigantocypris* was rather odd would not be an understatement: indeed it is one of the oddest of all abyssal animals. Sometimes a trawl-net comes up with

dozens, perhaps hundreds, of these pale orange peas. Up to 2.5 cm in diameter, *Gigantocypris* is aptly named, since its nearest relatives are seldom more than three millimetres across. It is bivalved, like a mussel, and from between the valves extend bristly antennae which propel this appealing creature along. The mode of progression appears amazingly random, with much looping, tumbling, bumbling and rolling. It is, of course, hard to be certain that some of this crazy movement is not a result of being trawled to the surface. To add to the weird effect, each ostracod (for this is Giganto-cyprid's group name) has a pair of 'headlamps' which biologists have always assumed to be eyes and yet which seem to have no lens or retina. The visible part of the 'eyes' is simply the two reflectors. These reflectors, true to nature's most devisive ways, are not spherical, concave reflectors, but parabolic, concave reflectors. For some time, biologists looked hard for a retina-like object at the focal point of the reflectors. It was finally recognized, transparent though it was. Strangely, these eyes seem only to collect light, not truly focus it, and this they do through a thickened rim of the valves, a section of their anatomy far from suited to acting as a window. One cannot help wondering exactly what it is that *Gigantocypris* sees, especially since it is known that adults are found at depths of at least 1,000 metres.

When *Gigantocypris* was first studied in detail it was invariably noticed that in the region of the brood chamber a rather vermiform parasite was to be seen wriggling around. One end of the worm was vaguely bottle-brush-like and often jostled around the eggs within the brood pouch. It is now recognized that the parasite is in fact a modified appendage of the creature, which in some way is associated with brooding activity.

Adaptive radiation
Amongst the enormous group of jointed-limb animals, the crustacea, with which much of the remainder of this chapter is concerned, are some spectacular instances of the phenomenon of adaptive radiation. A glance over a typical catch from a depth of 1,000 or more metres reveals a wealth of colour contrast, size contrast and design contrast and most is attributable to the crustacean content: deep red mysid shrimps and acanthephyran prawns, maybe 15 cm long; brilliant gold and orange, yellow and red, bright vermilion or pale pink copepods, with antennae nearly 5 cm from tip to tip; glassy transparent, or speckled, or orange and yellow amphipods – perhaps the most ubiquitous animal group within the deep oceans, with representatives present at all depths.

One of the amphipods, *Phronima* by name, deserves special mention, and is a special favourite of mine. *Phronima* is renowned for its house-building. These crystal-transparent amphipods feed particularly upon sea squirts, not the sessile rock-clinging type, but the mobile pelagic, and often colonial types, like those in Chapter 5. Pelagic sea squirts or salps swim by a reciprocating 'jet engine' and it is into this engine that *Phronima* swims and then eats the still-living sea squirt, from the inside. After devouring all the soft parts of the salp, the amphipod is left surrounded

236

236. Bottom-living poly-chaete worms probably feed on brittlestars and other polychaetes. Much of the benthic fauna depends, ultimately, upon a rain of dead carcasses from above.

237. Common though many benthic decapods are, because they enter the bottom trawl with a heavy load of ooze or shell gravel, they rarely show signs of life at the surface.

238. Benthic snapper shrimps from over 2,000 metres depth seem to differ little from those found close inshore. The shallow water species are invariably burrowers or live within sponges.

237

238

239

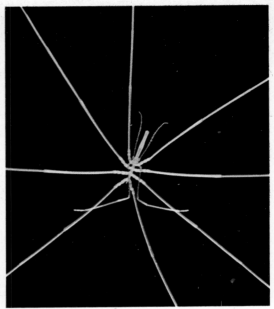

240

239. Though dredged from 2,000 metres depth, and therefore living in a world of total darkness, this bottom-living squat lobster shows few structural adaptations to its abyssal habitat.

240. Sea spiders or pycnogonids must have the smallest bodies in the world. The minute peg is the proboscis, while the virtually non-existent pin-head is the abdomen. Legs, however, may span 25 cm.

by the tough, but still-transparent, husk of tunicin. This it modifies to form a barrel, open fore and aft, and with a final shape peculiar to the species of *Phronima* and salp in question.

This macabre activity seems to be conducted by the female amphipods, and in time eggs, or hatchling amphipods, are deposited as a saddle on the inner wall of the barrel. Here they remain and grow while a respiratory flow of water passes over them. With advancing age comes the spirit of adventure, and juvenile *Phronima* start to stray from their brood site. Eventually, of course, they leave the parental home for good.

The eyes of an adult *Phronima* are a further feature of wonder in an animal already beset with extraordinary habits and adaptations. It has compound eyes, like most crustacea and insects, but unlike most, it has four, not two, of them. Each pair of eyes is situated on the side of the head. The outer eye and inner eye of each pair are actually in contact with each other, but here the similarity ceases. The outer eye is surrounded by a lozenge-

shaped ball of eye-facet lenses commanding an enormous field of view – perhaps 270 degrees. The eye next to it, and on its inner border, subtends enormously elongated ommatidia, or eye cones, each surmounted by a facet lens. These eye elements seem to look, as it were, through the creature's own head. The collective effect of these extended facets is to produce an enormously enlarged and domed head of almost crystalline appearance. *Phronima* are indeed strange animals.

If many, or most, mid- and deep-water animals arrive at the surface in a poor state of health, then those dredged off the bottom arrive at the surface in a very much worse state. The techniques of bottom dredging naturally scuff up a lot of bottom sediment and encrusting growth. This causes acute abrasion and asphyxia. For this reason, very, very few benthic (bottom-living) species survive the ascent. In general, the bottom-dredging techniques are, simply for physical reasons, unable to sample really deep water. It is therefore not surprising that many of the species so far discovered differ little from those known from deeper coastal stretches.

And so the mysteries of the deepest waters remain – and the fishy stories crop up with a fair degree of regularity. One which I know to be true, having seen the evidence, concerns an American biologist who used to experiment with remote photography at extreme depths, of creatures attracted to bait cans. These cans were, in one series of experiments, lowered to within a metre or two of the ocean floor in water of nearly 2,000 metres depth. Sequential flash photographs were taken and, in one series of shots, a large object was seen to black out the picture. By careful analysis of these shots it was possible to assess the dimensions of the animal responsible. The theory is that it was a deep-water shark of very considerable size – and by this I mean a shark, if shark it was, with a breadth across the head in excess of a metre! Heaven only knows what lies in the ocean depths: a long, long time must pass before man can really claim to have discovered all the secrets of his planet.

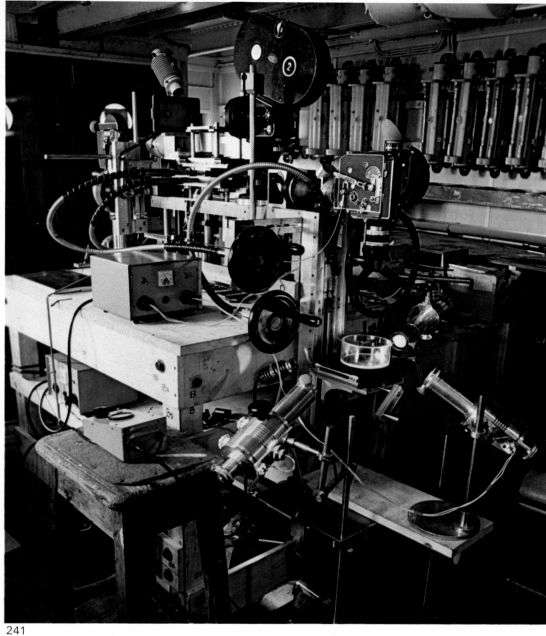

241

241. Filming anything at high magnification at sea is not easy. The specially modified Dark Field Optical Bench Mk. III enabled, for the first time ever, the photographing and filming of living material within minutes of it reaching the surface.

242, 243. Viewed through an owl-eye image intensifier, a benthic coral, seen in torch light, shows a branching lobed outline. When the torch is extinguished, the coral bioluminesces with its own energy.

242   243

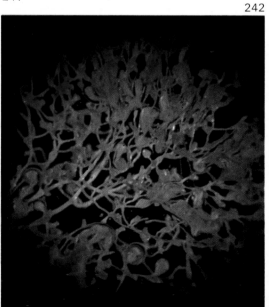

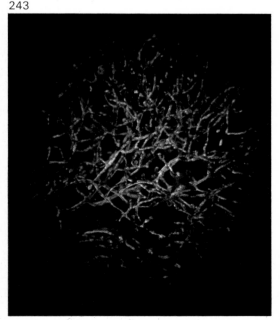

Chapter 7

The Oceanic World You Never See

In New York there is a famous jewellers called Tiffany's. Everyone knows of it. Its lure has been immortalized in Truman Capote's book, in which Holly Golightly had breakfast there, as well as in more than one popular song. But I would lay odds that one's admiration for the beauty of those crystal diadems would pale into insignificance when compared with the 'jewellery' in another famous New York establishment: the American Museum of Natural History. The exhibits displayed in the marine microbe section of the invertebrate hall would undoubtedly take one's breath away. The jewellery items are the myriad siliceous skeletons of oceanic radiolarian protozoa, or single-celled animals, belonging to the amoeba family. The specimens on view to the public are enlarged one and two thousand times in glass, and they were all blown with consummate skill by a German immigrant to the USA before the Second World War.

Glass was the artist's chosen medium because the real things are glass – animal glass. Silicon is absorbed from the sea and deposited with the amazing geometrical symmetry here depicted. The animals also colour their cellular tissue with brilliantly beautiful, or delicate and subtle pigments. These can match the radiance of diamond, the intensity of a ruby and the purity of an aquamarine. A certain Herr Müller, the glass-blower who designed and constructed all the magnified glass versions in the museum, has reproduced the radiolarian colours exactly as they appear in the live creatures. Not only has he constructed the outer shell of the skeletons, but through the pores and orifices of the outer envelope the observer can see the entire inner capsule which in life surrounds the nucleus. Müller's radiolarian work is reminiscent of old carved ivory chessmen of China: orbs within orbs, spheres within spheres, balls within balls – and every one visible through every other.

Rock from skeletal remains

The test (or skeleton) of so many of the micro-organisms of this, the ultimate world of the unseen, is exceedingly durable, therefore they remain as resilient sediments on the sea-floor of whichever ocean or sea they originate in. This process has been going on almost since time began. A number of Cambrian rock formations are believed to be based upon the skeletal remains of marine microbes.

A little nearer our time, but still several hundred million years ago, the skeletons of many species of marine foraminifera were starting to amass in the initial stages of formation of the White Cliffs of Dover. When one considers that ten or more foraminifera could sit comfortably on the full stop on a page of newsprint, the number of these tiny creatures that must exist in our seas seems almost impossible to comprehend. A cubic millimetre might contain between 500 and 1,000 foraminifera if they were stacked edge to edge. A cubic centimetre would by that reckoning contain up to a million individuals. The entire present massif of the White Cliffs would contain a greater number of these tiny creatures than could be represented in this book in terms of numerals.

Photographing detail in a radiolarian

To return to the first topic of this chapter, most of the radiolarian species possess long tapering spines as perfect in their lines as any rapier. The spines give these tiny animals a star-like quality, and just as a star often seems to radiate one beam of light further than another, so some radiolaria have one or more spines larger than the others. One species, depicted on page 110, has two very large spines which grow equally and oppositely. Other species subtend delicately curved spines from the rims of what can best be described as goblets with holes in them. The bases of the spines may expand into paddle-like extensions or be fused with a central capsule. This capsule may either directly contain the nucleus or contain a second capsule, which in turn contains the nucleus. All such capsules – like the goblet – are perforated with perfectly symmetrical, often graduated holes, and it is through these that the cytoplasm of the cell gently streams. In life it is just possible to see very fine filaments of cytoplasm radiating from the main capsule between the spines. The granules which are always present in the cytoplasm stream slowly out and back along these filaments, or filopodia.

A few years ago, while filming marine plankton species in the eastern Atlantic, we tried hard to expose cine film in such a way as to register these filopodia, that is, by purposely attempting to overexpose it. Even so, when we received the film

244. Clusters of star-like radiolaria gently tangle as drifting currents bring groups of the microscopic organism together in the subtropical waters of the Atlantic.

245. Even when magnified 800 times, little of the inner cell detail is visible in a radiolarian. Colouration often results from the presence of symbiotic chlorophyll-containing algal cells.

246. Most radiolaria have radiating silicon spines. From between these spines extremely fine cytoplasmic strands convey micro-organisms to the inner cell mass, which in this species harbours algal cells.

247. With what appears to be a siliceous perforated outer case and a lobed inner cell mass, this protist has so far defied nomenclature. Internally it resembles a foraminiferan and externally it seems to be a radiolarian.

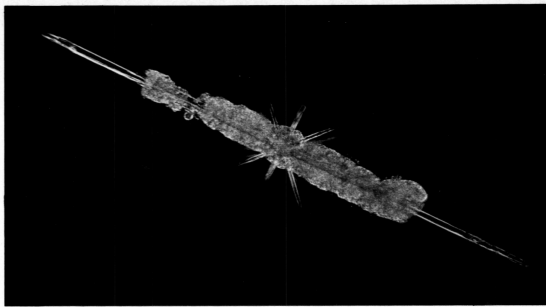

245

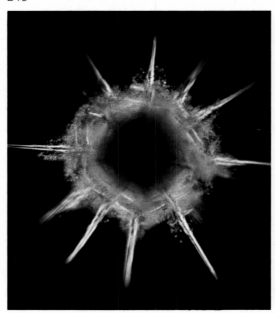

246

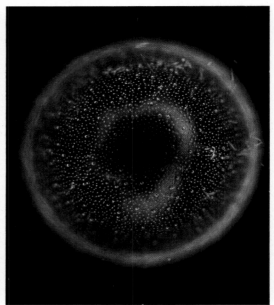

247

back from the labs, we were very disappointed, since nowhere had these delicate strands registered. Even on our stills films we had failed to allow sufficient overexposure of the main part of the radiolarian to show us the filopodia. About six months later I was editing part of our cine film, when I noticed that there were some very hot flash frames. (For those not familiar with cine film, a flash frame is one which receives a longer time exposure than intended, simply as a result of the camera slowing down when it is coming to the end of a shot. The same thing can happen as the camera works up to full speed, at the start of a shot.) It was immediately apparent that the flash frames in question, which were well overexposed, showed something more than the correctly exposed frames alongside. Closer inspection revealed just what we wanted – namely, correctly exposed filopodia. The rest of the radiolarian was hopelessly overexposed, but here, on one single frame from among the thousands, was the minute detail we required.

On the same filming project we also came upon two more species of radiolarian, each with something unusual about them. The two-spined species mentioned earlier was yellowish-green in colour and at least three other species had a distinct yellow tinge to their main cell mass. Since the trip, we have learned that the colour results from the presence of symbiotic algal cells in the cytoplasm.

Adjustable buoyancy tanks

The second unusual species of radiolarian was one which seemed to be a perforated glass ball, with minute spicules on the outer surface, encapsulating a radiating cytoplasmic network which seemed to emanate from an opaque mass of triple-spheres or quadruple-spheres, closely resembling a *Globigerina* foraminiferan (see page 115). The glassy outer capsule seems to define this species as radiolarian, while its inner contents seem to make it a chalky-based foram.

Earlier, the means by which most radiolaria produce relatively dense siliceous skeletons was

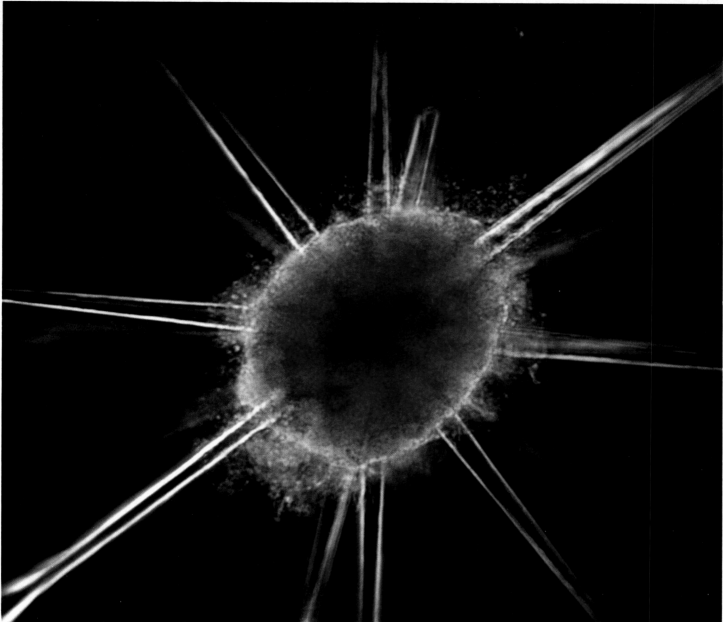

248

described. It is remarkable that the radiolaria manage to float near the sea's surface though themselves not endowed with any swimming ability. It seems that the outer frothy layer that covers most, if not all, radiolaria contains an ingenious hydrostatic device. Within the froth, large carbon dioxide-saturated vesicles of water appear and these act as a series of buoyancy tanks. In less clement weather, these vesicles are emptied and the little creatures sink slowly into calmer waters. But calmer, deeper waters are less well lit and, as stated earlier, most planktonic creatures depend upon their ability to remain within the upper photic zone of the sea. So, somehow, the radiolaria must prevent themselves remaining at any great depth. This they do by forming new vesicles which, literally like a gas-filled balloon, gently raise them to the surface again. Their presence at the surface is almost certainly more important for the survival of their symbiotic algal partners, found within the outer layers of their cell cytoplasm, than for their own well-being.

The main distinguishing feature between a radiolarian and a foraminiferan is just the fact that one bases its skeletal parts upon the mineral silicon, or *strontium*, and the other bases it upon calcium. A web-like, ramifying cytoplasm also typifies forams.

Foram-built rock
Not until we had filmed microplankton on Bermuda did we appreciate just how important foraminifera are. We did not realize, for instance, that the warm seas around Bermuda abound with forams. Nor did we realize that the rock from which Bermuda is compounded is to a large extent comprised of forams. One of the commonest species, occurring in every plankton haul we ever made there, was a bright orange, tiered-cone foram. Without fail, every single haul contained a dozen or more. Like all the species we found in Bermuda, this little chalky creature seemed to possess a flotation device. We trawled always in the topmost fathom of water and invariably be-

248. Magnified more than a thousand times an acanthometran radiolarian displays such an incredible intensity of colour it could truly be termed a gem of the sea. In death only the dagger-like spines settle to the sea bed.

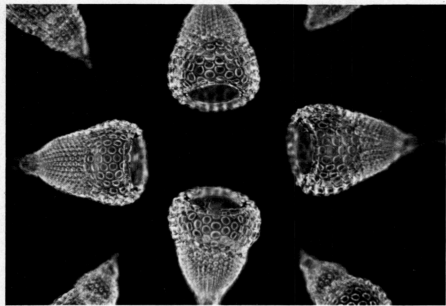

249

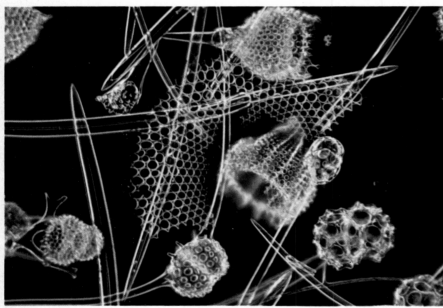

250

249. More than a century ago microscopists prided themselves on their ability to arrange, with symmetry and design, creatures as small as the goblet-like radiolarian tests.

250. Radiolarian skeletons litter the sea floor in some latitudes, and a sample viewed under dark-field illumination reveals a host of species that contributed to the ooze.

251. From apparently crushed radiolarian deposits, some fine specimens can, with patience, be extracted. Victorian microscopists specialized in this sort of preparation.

251

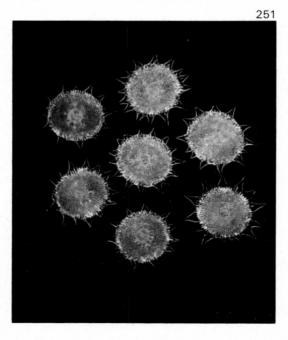

yond the reef: that is, in water in excess of 20 metres deep. In our viewing and sorting dishes these species had all, without exception, sunk passively to the bottom and remained there. Yet we were catching them *floating* in over 20 metres of water. We have taken up this point with several marine biologists and as yet we have found no satisfactory solution. When reading of foraminifera in textbooks we had assumed that they were furnished with flotation devices of some sort. Yet close observation provided absolutely no evidence for this. It is of course fair to say that many planktonic animals end up lying on the bottom of the receptacle in which they are placed. But in our experience, only the forams sink like stones and never rise again. Even the radiolaria soon waft upwards from the bottom at the slightest current. Possibly, these foram species attain neutral buoyancy some way beneath the surface, a shallow laboratory dish not being deep enough to permit this point to be reached. On many occasions in Bermuda, I must confess, we did see forams with what appeared to be a gas bubble within the lattice-like shell. Rightly or wrongly, we assumed that these bubbles were artefacts arising from rough treatment in the trawl-net. So, for us at least, it is still something of a mystery.

Black tide

Like the radiolaria, the forams also ramify their cytoplasmic tissue through pores in the calcareous test and they also send out radiating thread-like filopodia, but these intermesh in the form of a web. None of the photographs of forams on these pages has captured these fine structures, in spite of the facts that many of the species depicted were photographed alive and that the structures were fully visible through the viewfinder of the camera. In life, not only can one see the threads, but the cytoplasmic granules and inclusions can be seen to stream within them. The impression conveyed is of a central factory with a series of radiating conveyor belts carrying products and supplies to and from it. Foraminifera seem to ensnare minute life forms and it is quite possible that bacteria and small flagellates are their main food source. When one considers how abundant forams are in the tropics and subtropics, it serves to emphasize doubly just how prolific are their almost submicroscopic victims.

The abundance of forams in a place like Bermuda was certainly a revelation to those of us who were engaged upon that particular filming project. Not only did every single plankton haul that arrived aboard include dozens of forams, but on close inspection we rapidly found that a high percentage of the Bermudan beach sand, as well as that of the consolidated rock which forms the basis of this entire Atlantic mountain (for that is what Bermuda is), was foraminiferous in origin. There was, furthermore, a rather spectacular demonstration of this 'living' sand on one occasion while we were there. One particular morning tide left a dark and rather broad strand line on the white-hot beach. The blackness turned out to be the result of hundreds of thousands of almost black, pinhead-sized forams. The explanation for such a tidal stranding eludes us.

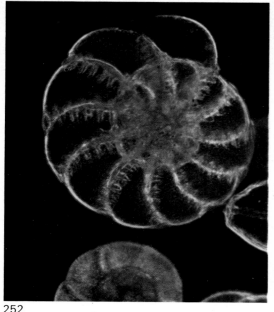

252

253

252. Whereas the skeleton of radiolaria is based upon silicon, that of foraminifera is based upon calcium. This does not prevent them displaying grades of symmetry equal to those of other protists.

253. Perhaps resembling snails rather than microscopic protists, many foraminifera increase their size by adding chambers. Cytoplasmic strands ramify within and around the test, but seldom show at normal exposure values.

254. Vast deposits of foraminiferan ooze lie beneath the warmer seas of the world. Such sediments, in time, form significant geological strata; for example, the White Cliffs of Dover are comprised largely of foraminifera.

254

Although great stress has been laid upon the fact that the creatures described in this chapter are small, it would be misleading not to point out that there are some forams of a considerable size. In the prehistoric past, many have been several centimetres across. However, though we have classed forams as protists, it is now known that many are multinucleate. It is not certain, however, whether this arose from colonies of cells joining their cellular tissues while retaining discrete nuclei, or from a sort of reproductive process in which offspring remain welded to the parent.

Cross-fertilization among foraminifera

In Chapter 3 there appeared a brief discussion, in passing, of the phenomenon of 'alternation of generations', that biological process whereby an organism divides its life, and its activities, into a sexual phase and an asexual phase. This dual life-style was first mentioned in connection with coelenterates, in which the sexual phase is usually associated with a pelagic medusoid stage and the asexual phase is associated with a sessile hydroid phase. In the foraminifera too, the same sort of phase alternation occurs. Hence many foram species are dimorphic, that is to say, they occur in two forms. Because the two morphs differ in the size of their first-formed calcareous chamber, they are known as microspheric and megalospheric forms. The microspheric form has a small central chamber and is multinucleate for most of its life. It reproduces asexually by multiple fission. It is left to the megalospheric form to ensure the survival of the species in evolutionary terms, since it is only this form that reproduces sexually. Uninucleate for most of its existence, the megalospheric form eventually becomes multinucleate, with each nucleus entering a motile flagellate gamete. These gametes swim freely and presumably mix with others arising from different megalospheric individuals. In this way, cross-fertilization is achieved and the hybrid vigour of the race ensured.

The importance of foraminifera in geological

255

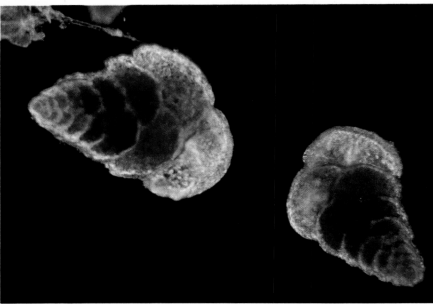

256

255. Reflected light shows up the thousands of minute foramina particularly well. In death, they allow protists to be made into excellent water filters; in life, cytoplasmic feeding strands radiate through these pores.

256. In Bermuda a bright orange species enters every plankton haul taken over the reef. It is characterized by long feeding strands of cytoplasm which constantly stream from the join between the two largest chambers.

investigation should not be overlooked, despite the fact that this book is intended to deal essentially with living material. The good geologist, and more particularly the palaeontologist, not only knows his fossil forms, but also has a good working knowledge of modern-day living organisms and their habits. This appreciation of live material helps him to determine much more about conditions many eons ago, when the particular fossils he is studying lived. This information is, in turn, of considerable help to fellow geologists working upon other topics within the same area.

Perhaps more than any other factor, fossil forams have helped geologists and engineers determine, site and put into effect high-productivity oil wells around the world. Because forams are small enough and plentiful enough to return reliably to the surface in deep-probe cores, they are an excellent index fossil. In exploitation of an oil-bearing rock series, one species was successfully used to trace the valuable rock layers from Nebraska to New Mexico. Another species was

used to do the same for a rock formation stretching from Cuba to Alabama and on to eastern Mexico. These index fossils are so important to the oil industry that all major oil companies have in-house foram specialists, to report upon and identify species found in both surface, subaquatic and subterranean investigations.

Forams as aids to research

How forams are used to guide geologists and engineers in their quest for oil is best demonstrated by considering a series of cores taken over, let us say, an 80-km transect. If the abundance of benthic forms increases along the transect it indicates progress towards shallow warm seas. The series can be further traced to indicate a primaeval shoreline. Comparisons between species existing then and now may tell the geologist that in one area a cold-water current restricted the abundance to a narrow inshore belt, or that in another existed a lagoonal sea so calm and tranquil that foram tests settled to the bottom, when dead, at a great rate. Furthermore, because some foram species produce tests into which they incorporate nearby shell gravel or sand particles, these species tell the geologist even more about the conditions which prevailed several hundred million years ago: he can determine a great deal simply by studying a $7\frac{1}{2}$-cm-diameter core sample.

The first recorded undisputed forams are agglutinated species from the middle Ordivician rocks of Oklahoma. Moreover, there is strong evidence to suggest that fossil organisms from Pre-Cambrian rocks of northern France and Cambrian rocks of New Brunswick are primitive forams. There is no doubt though that forams of a diversity similar to that which we know today have flourished on earth ever since the Devonian period.

As a final point of interest concerning the forams, there is one small but intriguing feature about certain fossil species which is worthy of note. Some forams can be collected in sufficient quantity to be used commercially. 'Foram ooze', as it is often called, is a wonderful water-filter, and for high-magnification film of microscopic protists we at OSF utilize a foram water-filter to provide us with water clean enough to prevent fogging of the water surrounding our subjects, under the extremely intense back-lighting we have to employ to film such small animals.

Light-giving dinoflagellates

Just as common as the forams in both Bermudan and Jamaican waters were, in our experience, the dinoflagellates. As a group, these half plant, half animal organisms play a vital role within the ecology of the plankton community. Besides this, dinoflagellates are strange and intriguing beings: time taken to study them is usually repaid with interest.

If it were not for the fact that our first example, *Noctiluca*, is rather anomalous in its design, a brief taxonomic definition of the word 'dinoflagellate' would have been appropriate here. Suffice it to say for the moment that most species have two whip-like flagella which beat within two grooves, usually arranged at right angles to each other. Most dinoflagellates have tough exteriors and many contain

257

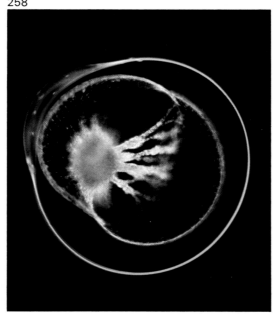

257. Unlike most forams the warm water species *Globigerina* has calcareous spicules similar to those of a radiolarian. These spines are presumably protective. Often they entangle drifting debris, which could be a feeding adaptation.

258. This globose species is a common, though strangely atypical, dinoflagellate of the Caribbean. A Swedish marine biologist told us its name, but unfortunately we lost the note we made of it!

plant-like photosynthetic pigments. In fact, the group of organisms now under discussion is that which comprises part of the planktonic 'grass' of the sea and is a group which is also frequently responsible for marine bioluminescence. Most people have seen or heard of the experience of midnight bathers discovering that moving their fingers and hands through the seawater could cause it to glow. In Chapter 5, a very spectacular instance in the north Atlantic was described. On that occasion copepods were responsible. A rather large dinoflagellate, however, is just as often the causative agent, especially around southern British coasts. The species is named after its habits and is aptly called *Noctiluca*. Millions of these globular little protists collect at the surface of the sea from time to time, usually during warmer summer months, and it is at this time that almost any disturbance will cause light to be emitted. A breaking wave will glow blue-green, a splashing fish will glitter like a tiara and an outboard motor will leave 'vapour' trails like an airliner. As early as

Easter we have collected and filmed *Noctiluca* in the Menai Straits, near Bangor.

There is one dinoflagellate which we often found, both in Jamaica and Bermuda, and for something like four years we had no idea it was a dinoflagellate. In fact it was after a film lecture I had given at Bangor (before the *Noctiluca* haul took place) that a visiting Swedish marine biologist identified the species as a dinoflagellate. (In the talk I had mentioned our uncertainty as to its identity and ventured to suggest that it could be an egg.) A week later I had lost the paper with the names of the Swedish biologist and of the dino-flagellate species. To this day it has not been re-named for us, and yet it is certain that many a marine biologist knows it. The species in question seems to have even less evidence of the dino-flagellate flagella than *Noctiluca*. Most of the cell is occupied by a tracery of cytoplasm around an invariably yellow nucleus. In *Noctiluca* a strange, prehensile tentacle has developed. It is said that this is not one of the flagella that has become modified. Certainly one flagellum remains present in *Noctiluca*. In our unknown Caribbean species this is not the case.

When our 'mystery' dinoflagellate divides, it does so by binary fission, but the outer envelope seems not to constrict and part into two offspring until all the cytoplasm and nuclear division is complete. It seems indeed that the outer case of this species is isolated from the cell contents. The cytoplasm is always surrounded by a well-defined membrane which always seems to float free within the outer case. This case is possibly a siliceous coat. As a spherical cover it seems to be fairly tough, but once dented, like a roughly handled ping-pong ball, it is a lot less tough and the relative strength of a radiolarian spine is clearly indicated in one of the plates.

Plants like anchors

Of all the dinoflagellates that inhabit this planet's seas, the commonest and most important must be *Ceratium*. This microscopic plant looks like a minute sea anchor. Many species exist, and the length and shape of the three prongs determine the type in question. Chains of these dino-flagellates may arise from simple division of the cell. Seldom, however, does the chain attain more than six individuals in all. Fragmentation of this chain presumably establishes new dinoflagellates, themselves capable of further division. At certain times of the year, single-celled plants increase so prolifically that 'blooms' may clog the plankton community and so, at such times, the animal population decreases. Certain species of dino-flagellates even synthesize toxins or poisons. The red tides of the American east coast, besides being a curious colour, also wipe out entire popu-lations of local fish, some of which would other-wise be commercially fished species.

Although we at OSF have not yet witnessed red tides, in Cornwall some years ago we did see a pink tide. One morning after a storm, when the breakers were exploding with such force that froth was accumulating, we noticed a pink tinge to the stranded bubbles. The next tide showed still fur-ther evidence of the same thing.

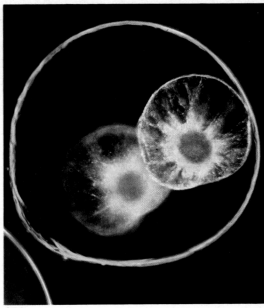

259

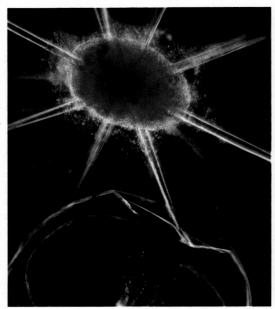

260

In general, tropical species of dinoflagellate (and planktonic organisms from many other groups) tend to be more spiny, or elongated, or feathery than their counterparts in colder waters. This appears to be an adaptation to prevent rapid sinking. In warm waters, objects may sink twice as fast as in Arctic or Antarctic waters, where water viscosity is much higher. Amongst dinoflagellates, especially those belonging to the pronged genus *Ceratium*, this elongation of spines is well demon-strated. The species depicted in the plate on page 117 is a good example of a warm-water form. There is now even some evidence that when *Ceratium* individuals drift from colder to warmer currents they can increase the length of their prongs to suit. This is a growth process and, of course, the higher temperatures assist this. There is also some evidence that dinoflagellates can shed some of their cellulose armour when passing from warmer to colder waters.

In recent years, research biologists have been taking very close looks at the remarkable flagellary

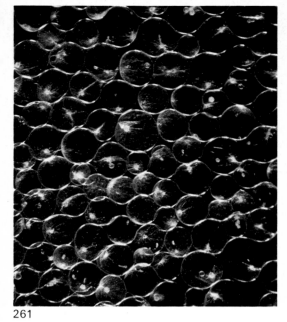

261

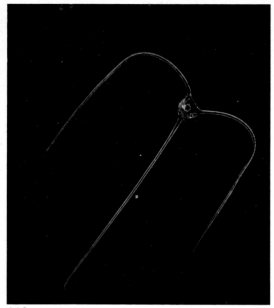

262

263

264

261. *Noctiluca* gives off its own light. This second atypical dinoflagellate is responsible for some of those phosphorescent seas encountered in warm summers on southern coasts. Water agitation stimulates the protists to bioluminesce.

262. *Ceratium* is perhaps the most important species of dinoflagellate in the sea. This widespread and diverse genus contributes a large part to the producer phytoplankton component of the sea's community.

263. Like washed grapes, two small single-celled algal spheres called *Halicystis* take their place on a Bermudan strand line. Locally known as sea bottles, this is one of the largest plant protists on earth.

264. A number 5 water-colour brush demonstrates just how enormous *Halicystis* is when it is remembered that most other creatures in this chapter are smaller than the diameter of a single bristle in the brush.

locomotor appendages of single cells. One might ask 'Why bother to look?' Well, from several standpoints flagellary movement is somewhat enigmatic. Firstly, flagella are not hairs or bristles, or anything like them: they are extensions of the cell – like the fingers of a rubber glove. Secondly, they are not and cannot be moved by muscles. (Muscles are made up of cells and here we are looking *inside* a single cell). Thirdly, even if muscles could exist inside flagella, it would be a sophisticated arrangement indeed if it were to produce the extreme flexibility and manoeuvrability shown by most flagella. An elephant's trunk can be twisted and contorted considerably, but it cannot then rapidly wag at the end, let alone along the whole length! By sectioning a flagellum and looking at it under the incredibly high magnifications afforded by the electron microscope, scientists can now tell us that nine bundles of contractile fibrils run the length of the structure, and lie just beneath its surface. Two more bundles are housed centrally. The manner in which these

'elements' operate is not well understood. We might postulate that the peripheral bundles manoeuvre the flagellum, while the central ones flail it, but this is only a hypothesis.

Gigantic plant cell

So often, it seems, the strand line can reveal a host of facts about the previous six to twelve hours. Detectives ferret around amongst human 'strand lines' such as ash-trays, litter, trouser turn-ups, down the backs of chairs and so on to piece together information about a person and his habits. Very similar techniques can be employed by a biologist scrutinizing a strand line. For eleven weeks, we walked the Bermudan tide-line twice a day, in the hopes of finding an odd little pelagic alga about which we had read in a book by William Beebe, of deep-sea fame. 'Sea bottles' is what the locals call these pelagic plants, and sea bottles is just what they look like. (The same name is occasionally applied to the Portuguese man-of-war.) The term 'sea-grape' would be an equally apt

265. Half-millimetre colonies of the filamentous alga *Trichodesmium* circulate within the Gulf Stream. The total biomass of this species present in the Atlantic must total hundreds of thousands of tonnes.

266. There must be thousands of diatom species. Enormous variety is displayed by the group, but whether chain-like, as this *Melosira*, or single, all diatoms seem to be encased by a base and lid.

267. Because most diatom species have extremely finely sculptured and perforated siliceous tests, they display a remarkable array of interference colours, when viewed under dark-field illumination. *Surirella*, seen here, is an excellent example.

name, but this same name is given to a herbaceous plant found growing on subtropical coasts. The object in question is the size and colour of a white grape, but is more translucent, and when lying on the coral sand, with the sun high in the sky, it acts like a lens and, as it were, sits on a plinth of brightness – brightness condensed by its own vegetable tissues. When we found our first halicystids, we were struck by the fact that their light-focusing properties gave them a miniature, but close, resemblance to the 12-cm-diameter green glass floats used by fishermen as net-floats.

When filming *Halicystis* we devised a sequence of intercut shots between the algal cell and its glass megamimic. The all-revealing shot, of course, concludes the sequence and shows that what has been assumed is just another glass float being picked up between, and dwarfed by, a finger and thumb.

It was as a result of filming the above *Halicystis* sequence that my back came near to collapsing! Towards the end of our eleven-week expedition to the small island of Nonsuch off Bermuda, I severely slipped a disc and shortly became confined to a horizontal existence for ten days. The straw that broke this camel's back was trying desperately to film *Halicystis*. After the initial disc displacement I was still able to hobble around. It was then we found our first large *Halicystis*. By this time my filming colleague, Sean Morris, had departed for the UK. A situation had therefore arisen which obliged me to have a go at completing the sequence. Much against the wishes of my distressed wife, I sallied forth with camera on to the beach. *Halicystis*, on a strand line, is rather demanding upon the cameraman with a damaged back, who obstinately wishes to achieve ultra-low-angle shots of the algal cell. Half stooping, half lying and half crying, I scrabbled around the beach trying hard to show the alga actually being stranded by an incoming wave. Predictably, a larger than normal wave swept the *Halicystis* away and up the beach and simultaneously threatened to soak the camera, so in an effort to track with the cell and more desperately, to rescue the camera from the water, I contorted my back into an agonising position. That was it. Ten days later I was still on my back in bed. Six weeks later I was still severely hampered by sciatic pains in both legs. It was later still before my wife forgave my recklessness.

Test-object extraordinary
Halicystis is one of the largest plant cells in the world. Fully the size of a grape, a large individual is second to no other plant cell for volume or bulk. For that reason, this surface-drifting protist alga is used by plant physiologists for certain aspects of research into plant cytology.

In complete contrast to the sea bottle is another protist alga, but this one assumes a filamentous outline and is called *Trichodesmium*. Hundreds of such algal needles associate to give rise to a ball of filaments. The finished result is very reminiscent of a woollen pompom made by winding wool around a circular card with a hole in the middle. When the wool has not been wound tightly enough a rather loose, shaggy ball results, which is very like *Trichodesmium*. This pin-hole-sized protist cluster

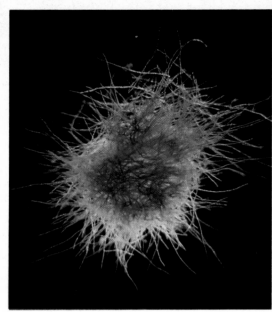

265

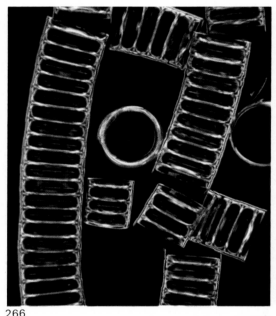

266

267

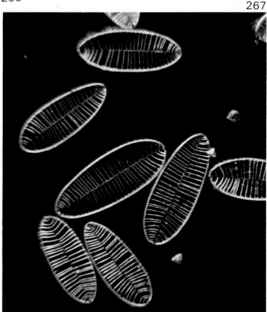

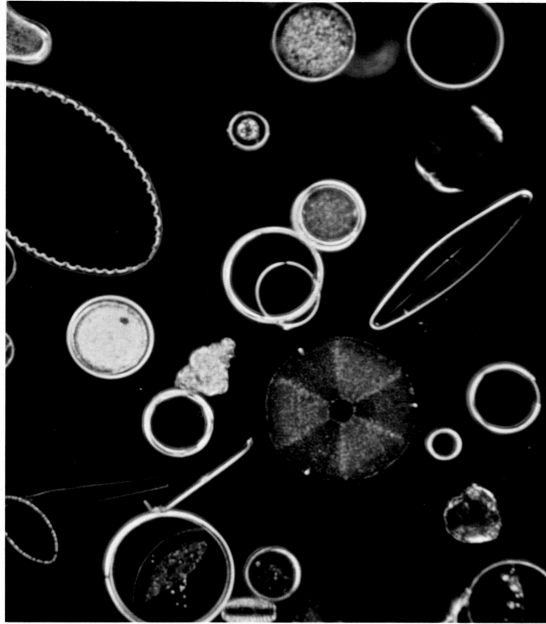

can occur in considerable quantities in the warmer seas of the world, and occasionally collects where two surface currents meet. They roll beneath the waves and give rise to scum-like windrows comprised of little other than the algae in question.

So much for vaguely plant-like protist plants! Now, to complete the picture, let us look at some amazing and very unplant-like protist plants, the diatoms.

It is perhaps fair to say that one of the characteristics of plants that appeals to man is their irregular yet conforming growth styles. No two oaks are the same, no two elms are the same, and yet they are unmistakably oaks and elms. A rose, for all its regular line, is never symmetrical, never a mathematical or geometrical exactitude. Even the regular and repetitive detail of a fern frond or a mimosa leaf, or the gills on the underside of a mushroom, lack any equational definition. Could plants be described as the most random life forms? If they could, then think again when we come to the protist plants called diatoms. These

incredibly minute plant cells could have easily originated from a computerized factory where their design was formulated by the cursor of a slide rule. As if to emphasize their role in the annals of high-precision science, some of the marine diatoms have managed to achieve for themselves the title of 'test object extraordinary'. The pores and striae and sculptured detail on the tough outer siliceous tests of these diatoms are still used, to this day, as resolution test objects for microscope objectives. Man, in his less than infinite wisdom and with his less than perfect technical skills, finds it hard to etch, engrave or photographically reduce a grid fine enough and small enough to act as a suitable test object. The genus most often used for test purposes is *Navicula*, and this diatom sports striae which are less than one ten-thousandth of a millimetre apart. Modern, high-quality microscope objective lenses can resolve 200 to 400 lines per millimetre, depending upon the quality of the lens and also the quality of the image required. (High-resolution lenses do not neces-

269. Victorian microscopists not only appreciated beautiful subject material, but also excellent presentation. The thought of manipulating *Actinocyclus* diatoms as seen here, measuring only 1/100 mm across, in poor light, is awesome!

270. The same microscopists also knew how to illuminate subjects for optimum effects. Most modern microscopists seldom achieve illumination capable of depicting *Actinocyclus* as in this and the previous plate.

271. Most of the animal biomass of the seven seas is directly dependent upon diatoms for harnessing the ultimate energy source — sunlight. This fact helps us to appreciate the extent of the total mass of diatoms.

272. Diatoms shown in this and the subsequent plate are still used by microscopists to test the resolving power of microscope objectives. Cellular sculpturings are fine, but irregular; hence multi-chromatic interference colours appear.

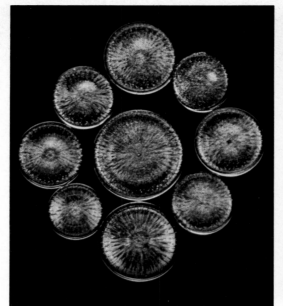

269

270

271

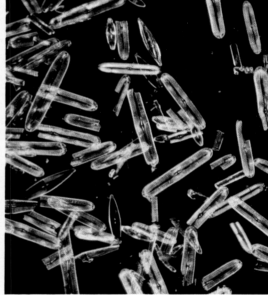

272

sarily carry very high definition or acutance values.)

It is because they carry these microscopic surface details that nearly all diatoms catch the light and display gaudy interference colours. Interference colours appear in a number of biological tissues and surface layers. The sheen on bird feathers is an interference colour. Moths and butterflies also often have a sheen on their wings and this too is produced by interference effects. The rainbow pattern on water, when oil has spilt, is an interference pattern, and so is the pale rainbow hue seen when two sheets of glass are pressed together. The lustrous colours of silk are usually interference variations on the basic dye used. So what then, exactly, is an interference colour, and what factors do the above examples have in common which produce this phenomenon?

Colour without pigment
The simple explanation of the colours is that when light passes through very closely-spaced slits, lamellae, pores, or layers of translucent or transparent materials of different refractive indices, it is scattered on leaving the slit or layer in question. The scattered light from one slit then reinforces or diminishes the wave form of that from the next. All interference colours are spectral, and therefore have a very pure and intense lustre. All seem to have a metallic sheen to them and being structural colours (no pigment being responsible for the colour) they can be removed by filling the slits, or pores, or layers with a liquid whose refractive index is different from the air or water with which the slits are usually filled. If, for instance, chloroform or ether is poured on to a burnished neck feather of a pheasant, all colour disappears; when the solution evaporates, however, the interference colour returns. In this instance the colours are produced by minute lamellae which sandwich a layer of air between themselves and the next lamella. The solution fills these air spaces and prevents interference.

All diatoms seem to show some degree of interference colour, but some do so only faintly. This

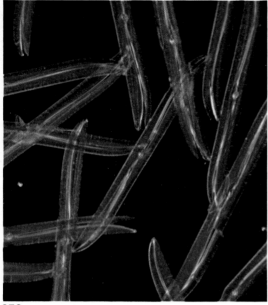

273

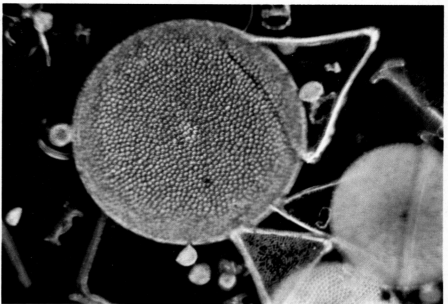

274

is another way of saying all diatom tests have pores and slits, though the function of these is not certain; however, it is known that diatoms move. This they do in a slow yet steady fashion, and many a biologist has pondered upon the mechanism. The box-like cells (for each diatom consists of a siliceous base over which a lid fits snugly) seem to have absolutely no sign of motility organs. It has been suggested that the pores and slits common to all diatoms hold the clue to diatom progression. Through these orifices, it is proposed, a stream of mucilage slowly passes. Either because of a slight hydrofuge property, or because of an equal and opposite reaction, such an emission could produce the slow gliding motion exhibited by diatoms.

At extremely high-powered magnification, it is possible to see a very rapid and spectacular cytomplasmic streaming within some diatoms. *Rhizoselenia* is a species of diatom which shows very marked internal streaming of the cytoplasm. This, however, may be a far cry from the mucilage stream mentioned above. Nonetheless, it does tend to indicate a level of metabolic activity capable of providing sustained though slow movements.

To solve the mysteries that surround one species of diatom would be to explain one of the natural phenomena of this world that to me, at least, is one of its seven wonders.

Paradoxical diatom

The first time I ever saw the species in question, I thought it was a minute grease-smear on the bottom of the petri dish. The last time I saw it, I was compelled to accept that several hundred thousand hectares of littoral debris, across the benthic and the drifting plankton layers of Westernport Bay, 64 kilometres south-east of Melbourne, Australia, were caused to heave gently as a result of its microbial activity. These microscopic plants were needle-shaped diatoms which curiously clustered in packs. Viewed from one angle they were like a pack of cards, but viewing the pack end-on would have revealed that the cards were

needles. Closer examination of these diatom packs revealed that every needle in the pack could, and invariably did, slide upon its neighbour. First it slid one way, then the other. The needle in the centre of the pack seemed to act as a locus around which the others operated, for when a pack first extended so far as to look like a hair and then contracted, at the point of maximum contraction, the whole pack often seemed to turn or spin around its own centre, so an east/west-moving pack suddenly changed to a north/south-moving pack.

To date, no satisfactory explanation has been put forward to explain how or why such movement is executed. What can be the advantage to the diatom? Does it help to jostle the individuals to the better-lit surface of the debris in which it sometimes lives? Why on earth would a microscopic plant evolve this amazingly mobile and flexible type of movement especially when all its relatives, which number in the thousands, have apparently never evolved any similar mobility? The name of the curious diatom is apt: it is called *Bacillaria paradoxa*. *Bacillaria*, with one or two very close relatives such as *Nitschia*, is the only diatom to show this ridiculous ability. To find a reason for the movement is hard enough. To explain how the moment is achieved is harder still. Perhaps it is a mechanism which could give us a clue as to how vertebrate muscle fibrils move one against the other. Could the movement be a chemical ratchet mechanism, with chemical linkages being alternatively made and broken, and if it is . . . why is it?

As if to add a touch of glamour to the already attractive spectacle *Bacillaria* displays a series of band-like interference patterns, and so, when the pack of cells is closed, a very regular decorated plaque is the result. As soon as it starts to elongate, the bands lose their continuity across different cells, and so the change of shape is also accompanied by a very marked change in pattern and colour as well.

Last in the succession of strange phenomena within this chapter are two examples of association between diatoms and other organisms. The first example is of a diatom which is parasitic upon

273. Magnified 400 times, *Pleurosigma* just begins to show the fine striae that are responsible for the interference colours. Most diatom species show a mid-nodal point in their siliceous tests.

274. Pores in the test are believed to permit a stream of mucus to pass around the cell and create the gliding process. Although this has been observed for years, it has never been satisfactorily explained.

275. A typically geometrical species of diatom known as *Triceratium* from the southern Atlantic is shown here.

276. The siliceous tests of diatoms are durable and skeletal remains form deposits of considerable magnitude. Diatomaceous earth is the name given to the deposit, which in parts of the world has agricultural value.

277. The cosmopolitan *Bacillaria paradoxa* must surely be another contestant for one of the seven wonders of the natural world. No one knows why, or how, its cells slide side by side.

278. Symbiosis, on a miniature scale, is exemplified by a Caribbean marine vorticellid ciliate, which establishes itself between the spines of a *Biddulphia* chain diatom. The ciliate propels; the diatom protects.

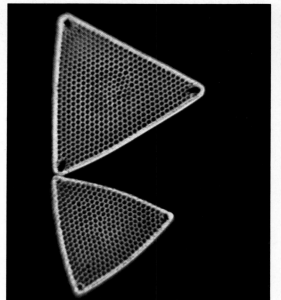

275

276

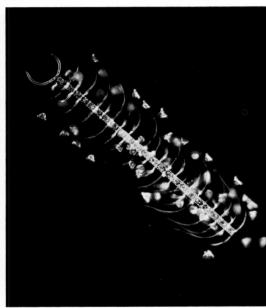

277

278

a calcareous alga. In fan-like array, the diatoms cluster around the algal branch-tips. The term 'parasitic' may be a misnomer, for no one is too sure of the exact life-style of these diatoms. The same applies to the clusters of yellow diatoms which are frequently found attached to the bodies and antennae of copepods. At times, a copepod can be so smothered with these diatoms as to be unrecognizable. Perhaps the diatoms are, strictly speaking, only attached to the copepod, but it has been seriously suggested that they take something more than just support.

Our final diatom is a species common to the north Atlantic. The gem in this case is *Biddulphia*, and it is characterized by forming chains of cells, end to end, and with each cell subtending recurved spines. In Jamaica we frequently came upon this species in our daily plankton hauls. Peering with tired eyes into a binocular microscope one day to review the haul, I noticed one of these chain diatoms gently 'burn' across the field of view. 'Burn' describes its progress well, because

it had the ease of flight of a spacecraft. What could conceivably propel such a colony of plants? Then I realized. Lying snugly between *Biddulphia's* spines were numerous ciliated vorticellids – indeed, a whole colony. So here we had an animal colony living on a plant colony, and it was the ciliary feeding currents set up by the vorticellids that were propelling the tiny craft. The diatom received advantage from the progress by being rotated through sunlit waters, while the vorticellids were protected from danger by being able to contract between the spines of the diatom. Altogether, the association seemed to be a good example of symbiosis, but on a minute scale.

Incidentally, *Biddulphia* is a diatom species about which there is some mystery. Until about 1903 it was unknown in European waters, having hitherto only been found in Indo-Pacific waters. Maybe it had just been missed, but so much phytoplankton study was undertaken at the end of the 1800s that this seems unlikely. It seems possible that the species, which is very temperature-

279

and salinity-tolerant, was brought to the mouth of the Elbe (where it was first recognized) in the ballast water of a trading-vessel. Before many years had elapsed the species had spread around the British Isles and was reported from Plymouth in 1909. This same find, incidentally, may add strength to the belief that the prevailing currents within the English Channel occasionally reverse.

Conclusion

Much of this book's anecdotal and photographic information was gleaned from a series of biological filming expeditions to various parts of the world, including a twelve-week trip to Jamaica in 1967 during which three 50-minute television films were made for the BBC. One of these, *The Living Sea*, concerned the little-known world of plankton.

Subsequent expeditions took OSF to Florida, the Wisconsin wetlands, the Great Lakes, Bermuda, South Australia and even into mid-Atlantic aboard a research vessel. From each excursion came a wealth of rich experience in aquatic investigation, from which these seven chapters are largely drawn.

Our sustained interest in the unseen world of water, both marine and fresh, has, I think, taught us one lesson. It is that however simple, however small, however primitive the creatures within any environment, we can nonetheless expect to find associations, relationships and dependencies as sophisticated and complicated as any we see in higher organisms. Lack of such examples in any one area is usually a reflection of man's lack of detailed knowledge, rather than of absence of the phenomena.

It is to be hoped that this book and its contents will inspire just a few more laymen or biologists to explore the unseen world of water, and that in doing so they will gain as much pleasure from their investigations as we have from ours.

279. Some species of diatom are believed to be parasitic. Here dense clusters of *Licmophora* smother the branches of a calcareous alga. Other diatoms appear to parasitize copepods.

Index

Acknowledgements

The author would like to thank many friends for their help and encouragement:
Leonard Small, Zoology Department, Oxford, for cheerfully and frequently supplying cultures of freshwater protists used in Chapter 1. Professor David Nichols of Exeter University and Dione and Alistair Gilmour of Melbourne, Australia for facilities, identification and help with the contents of Chapter 3, as well as hospitality which will long be remembered. David Wingate, Conservation Officer of Bermuda, for allowing eleven weeks of unique and privileged access to Nonsuch Island, thus making Chapters 4 and 5 possible. Professor Ivan Goodbody and 'Mr Murph' at the University of the West Indies Biology Department, Jamaica, for an incredible number of plankton hauls as well as advice and facilities provided for part of Chapter 5. Peter David, Peter Herring, David Shale, Martin Angel and Nigel Merrit of the Institute of Oceanographic Studies, Wormley for tolerating endless queries during six weeks at sea and so facilitating much of Chapter 6. To colleagues at OSF for photographic and anecdotal material: John Cooke for writing Chapter 3 and for supplying several plates in the same chapter as well as for his general help and humour. Gerald Thompson and Sean Morris for their help in the writing of Chapter 2. To Susi, the author's wife for her typing skills and her patience and forbearance, through ten months of evening work at home. To Hugh Falkus who, being a fellow 'aquaphile' and notable and gifted storyteller, did much to generate the will to complete the anecdotal nature of this book. And finally to three eminent biologists: Professor Sir Alister Hardy, Professor Niko Tinbergen, and Professor David Nichols, to whose encouragement and enthusiasm for all things small and watery the author owes so much.

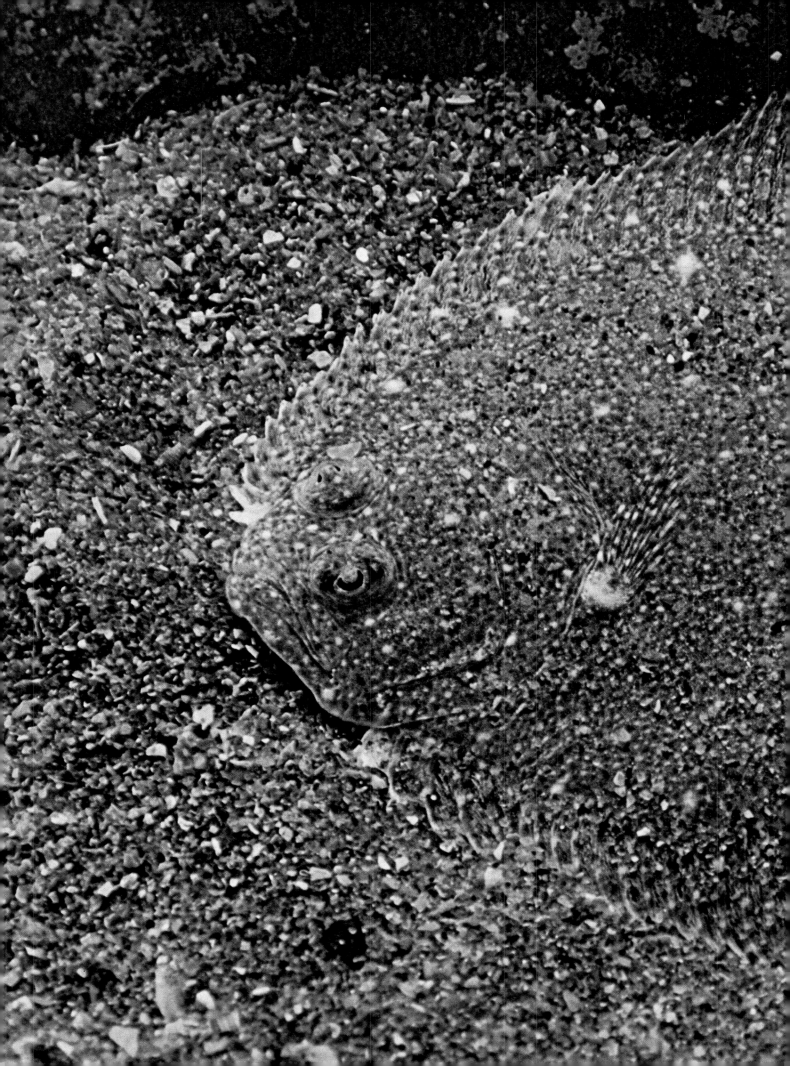